BORN BEAUTIFUL

How Counselling Theory
Can Enrich Our Parenting

Jane Teverson

First published by Free Association Books.

Copyright © 2020 Jane Teverson

The author's rights are fully asserted. The rights of
Jane Teverson to be identified as the author of
this work has been asserted by her in accordance with the
Copyright, Designs and Patents Act 1988

A CIP Catalogue of this book is available from
the British Library

ISBN: 978-1-911-38341-3

Typeset by
Typo•glyphix
www.typoglyphix.co.uk

Cover design by
Candescent

Printed and bound in England

For
Adam, Lucy and Ross

CONTENTS

FOREWORD

'...much mental ill-health and unhappiness is due to environmental influences which it is in our power to change.'
Bowlby

This book asks its reader to really consider the lives of the children in our care, and the long-term effect of the care we provide.

It's about children who have had their hearts broken by their parents or the people who have brought them up. We tend to think in terms of a broken heart when an adolescent or adult love relationship comes to an end. But this isn't the only way that a heart can be broken. Many adults are walking through their lives with a broken heart which they have carried since childhood, and this broken heart is crippling the best part of them and needs to find healing.

So this book isn't only asking you to consider the child in your care but also the child you once were. The child you carry with you. The wounded place in you that needs to be acknowledged and healed, if you are to lead a fulfilled and peaceful life.

'How is it that we know so much and don't "do" anything?'
Barry Stevens

INTRODUCTION

This book is the book I would have liked to have read before I had my children. So it will be simple. Nevertheless it is based on many years of study and work which began with A levels at the age of forty, a degree in philosophy, my training as a psychodynamic counsellor and my privileged work with clients. So much of the anguish which brings people into counselling has its roots in the discomfort and pain of early relationships.

On a more personal level, this book is based on the experience of being an unwanted child. Of being the mother of three beautiful children who I wanted to be a good mother to, but some 'thing' kept getting in the way. I knew the good mother was there and she did eventually win the battle. But the winning of this battle was a tough and close thing. It was also late in the day and I believe it could have been won sooner.

My hope is that this book will give its readers what I needed all those years ago. A true awareness of what is at stake in our relationship with our child. The simple things our baby needs from us (for their own sake and ours) to develop in a happy, well-balanced way. And for older people – hope. The realisation that it's never too late to be the parent you would have liked to have been, had circumstances been different for you, as re-parenting is a very real and valuable process. 'We can break out of our own patterns of childhood conditioning and free ourselves from the cycle of automatically – without regard to whether they're helpful or harmful – passing these patterns on to our children.' [1]

The important words to notice here are *we can* – and indeed we can break out of our own unhelpful patterns of childhood conditioning, but first we have to become aware of how that conditioning has impacted us.

There are, of course, situations that come along in life that simply cannot be avoided. However, there is a great deal projected onto babies, infants and children which could and should be avoided with what I call the three 'Cs': caring, compassion and common sense. And above all, with awareness of the far-reaching effects of what we are doing.

1

HOW COUNSELLING THEORY CAN ENRICH OUR PARENTING

A counsellor seeks to make available to her client:

> '...the respect of one human being for another and hope for
> the potentialities of this other person.'
>
> **Cassie Cooper**

A counsellor hopes that her client will come out of therapy with:

> '...the opportunity to love well, to work well, to play well,
> and to have some optimism for the future.'
>
> **Cassie Cooper**

The first quote talks about respect and this is the least that any adult can have for any child, whatever the circumstances. Respect and hope for the well-being of another person, particularly a child, costs nothing and yet it gives and makes possible everything.

The second quote is how we should all emerge from childhood. With the exception of the unavoidable – death, natural disasters or war – we should all emerge from the years of childhood 'with the opportunity to love well, to work well, to play well, and to have some optimism for the future'. This, quite simply, is every child's birthright. But we have to wonder why so many of us don't. Carl Rogers believed that when a client experiences the counsellor as empathic they can experience a fundamental shift towards psychic health which allows for a more authentic relationship with themselves, other people and every aspect of their life.

There is so much in the counselling theory that can make an important contribution to successful parenting. What can anyone involved with children in any way learn from the client/counsellor relationship that can help them give to children what they need from the start? Perhaps a look at what counselling seeks to achieve and how it seeks to achieve it will offer insights for the care of children, that will contribute to well-balanced and fulfilled adult lives, with less wasted potential and better outcomes for future generations.

For Rogers the quality of the relationship between the client and counsellor is an integral part of the healing process. In just the same way the relationship of the child to both parents is an integral part of the child's development. So from Roger's theory we can gain insights that can help the relationship between parent and child to be everything it could and should be.

INNER RESOURCES

Rogers saw it as his task to put the client back in touch with their own inner resources. Resources that allowed them authentic use of their capacity to be free to make choices and to be responsible for those choices. This *inner resource* is crucially important because its loss is psychologically crippling. With Rogers, the initial step towards reinstatement was to challenge the authority of the counsellor. The reason being that if clients were going to be able to explore and express themselves freely, the counsellor had to come to the session with an open, non-judgemental mind. In the same way, what I am doing throughout this book, is questioning the often intransigent authority of the parent. Of course parents must provide a safe containing space for their children to grow up in – that is a crucial foundation – but we don't need to portray ourselves as all-powerful and always right. It is just this attitude that can cripple the inner resources of our children. In fact, it can be a relief for the parent and the child if the parent can admit that they have made a mistake. After all, mistakes are part of life and learning to admit them and learn from them and move on is an important life skill for us to have ourselves and to teach our children. This alone could reduce the unnecessary and debilitating feelings of shame that get stored in young bodies.

TRUE SELF

To a certain extent, we are all composed of a *true self* and a *false self*. It is simply a matter of degree. What is important though is which of these 'selves' has the ultimate control of our lives. The true self is that part of us which as infants reaches out to explore our world. If that true self is met with acceptance and understanding, and hopefully love, we are able to reach a place of compromise with the world, where we still have a major shareholding in how our lives evolve. However, where our infant self has met with rejection, ignorance, negativity, restrictions and/or harshness, our true self withdraws. The part of us that instinctively reaches out to the world can become defeated. From this point forward, our false self negotiates the world for us, in our 'best' interests. On the outside, we can appear to be doing well enough. On the inside we sense that all is far from as it should be and that we are not living the life that is truly ours to live.

The true self longs to be seen, to be heard and to be accepted, first and foremost by ourselves. This is very often the cause of a midlife crisis, making it a very important and creative opportunity in our lives. It is our true self, calling us to wake up and live our own life. And it is this true self that the counsellor/client relationship can contact, empower and welcome into the world.

What counselling initially seeks to provide is an 'atmosphere' that allows for the telling of the client's 'story'. As the story unfolds, and if the time is right, there follows the gradual and gentle removal of defences. For many, the demands of childhood are such that, without realising it, our psychological, emotional and sometimes physical survival depends on how well we have built this false self. Our false self enables us to cope with the demands of parents, teachers, peers and society. These are authorities that we have to conform to but sometimes they can be too much for the true self inside us to cope with. Everyone has to do this to a certain extent but it is a matter of *degree*. The problem is that where circumstances are harsh or simply unreasonable, over a long period of time, the false self takes over. Who we really are is all but lost and with that loss goes the loss of all the potential selves that we could have *chosen* to be. Psychiatrist Dr. Brian Weiss in his book *Many Lives Many Masters* endorses this when he notes that the endless criticism of a parent can actually cause more emotional damage to a child than one traumatic incident. It's insidious because it hardly registers on the radar as it becomes part of the everyday experience of the child. This constant criticism can lead to a loss of confidence and seriously impact the self-esteem of a child and the adult they will one day become.

Counselling seeks to gradually put clients back in touch with that precious true self, sometimes called the *core* or *seed self.* Either of these words, core or seed, gives us an intimation of how deeply hidden this self can become under layers of conformity – but even more importantly, the limitless potential this self contains. However hidden it is though, it is only under extreme circumstances that it will completely give up the right to be heard, seen and appreciated. This need of the true self for expression sets up an inner conflict and to contain this conflict takes up a tremendous amount of energy. As clients regain 'permissible' contact with this true self, the freed-up energy allows for new growth in every sense: spontaneous, creative, life-affirming. They begin to experience and fulfil their potentiality for a well-balanced and satisfying life; a life of their choosing. So it follows that if children grow up in a spontaneous atmosphere, sensitively contained, loved and respected, from the outset their energy can be used to fulfil their potential 'to love well, to work well, to play well, and to have some optimism for the future'.

HONESTY

Carl Rogers believed that the successful outcome of therapy depended on how much a client could 'risk' to tell a counsellor. How much could he 'risk' to show of himself to the counsellor and still be accepted? How much could she 'dare' to tell the counsellor without rejection? In short, how *honest* could he be? There is a need in each of us to be honest and yet so often we learn as children that to be honest is to be condemned or to be misunderstood. How much 'dare' a client tell the counsellor? How much 'dare' a child tell his parents, carer, teacher? The more open and honest a child is able to be without fear, with that openness and honesty received in a compassionate and common sense way, whatever the circumstances, the more autonomous and responsible that child can and will become. And the more confident and successful in all types of relationships, not least and most importantly, in relationship with themselves. 'Children need time to grow, time to play. They need time to unfold the subtle essence of the self, their unique contribution to the whole. If the proper atmosphere is created during the early years – an atmosphere of love, patience, ordered activity and understanding, then the true nature of the child can flourish and grow. This is the birthright of every child.' [3]

If the right 'atmosphere' is so important we need to know how that right atmosphere is created. The answer is very simple: it is created by our attitude. In counselling, the attitude that the counsellor brings to the session will have a crucial influence on the outcome of the therapy. In just the same way, the right attitude to our children is of crucial importance to the outcome of their development. This is because babies and children are more sensitive to the emotional attitudes of those caring for them than anything else. Perhaps they know intuitively that their own health and safety is dependent on the emotional and psychological health of those caring for them.

EMPATHIC ACCEPTANCE

So what is this 'attitude' and what does it make available to the client and what would it make available to our children? The attitude that is so important is an attitude of *empathic acceptance.* What I understand by the words 'empathic acceptance' is that I accept the client's core/seed/soul self without reservation, separate from what he has done or become. There is a line from one of Philip Larkin's poems that puts it beautifully: 'On me your voice falls as they say love should, like an enormous yes' [4] and that is what I want to say from my heart and soul to the heart and soul of my client. It is a message of acceptance.

We know we are a mixture of what we inherit, our environment and nurture, but there is a part of us which is separate from all of this; we can call it the soul self, and this soul self is innocent and striving for expression. There is a line from a song that comes to mind, 'Return to yourself, return to innocence.' Our soul self is happy to accept what is good for us by way of inheritance, by way of environment and by way of nurture, but it is also striving to be its own self. And isn't it extraordinary that to be true to this soul self is made so difficult for us as children, by every injunction that is put on us to conform, to fit in – more often than not for the convenience of others?

Simply saying 'yes' to this self is the beginning of a process that will eventually allow for a healthy, autonomous and fulfilling life. And if it is important in the counselling relationship, how much more important it must be for the infant and evolving child. This 'yes' should be in place from the beginning. It is every child's birthright. Saying 'yes' in your heart to your child is crucial to your child's well-being throughout life. Tragically it can be difficult for some parents to say yes from the heart when they are themselves handicapped by early experiences of rejection. Which is why recognition of our own wounds and doing the healing work we need is so important, not only for ourselves but for the lives we touch.

THE CHILD'S EMOTIONS

If this empathic response is fundamental for a successful outcome in counselling, how much more important must it be in infancy, where all that the infant child has to go on is *what he feels*. These feelings are crucially important because for the most part they arise from preverbal emotions. The importance and legacy of these emotions is emphasised by Virginia Satir in her book *People Making* where she says that emotions have an impact on both our behaviour and our intelligence. (A reminder that emotional stability can be as important for a successful life as IQ.) So the way in which we respond to these feelings becomes of paramount importance.

Remember that all the infant and evolving child has are feelings that prompt his every move, and so invites, for better or worse, the responses he receives. Where the response to his infant self is at least predominantly kind, he can gradually develop a true sense of self. Where, however, he is met with impatience, harshness, hostility or any inappropriate response, panic sets in and his ability to make sense of himself and the world around him is compromised. (And it does amaze me how many of the clients I have worked with have said they are dyslexic which makes me wonder if this is yet another condition that is exacerbated by stress in infancy and childhood.) Inevitably, everyone's attempts at primary individuation are compromised to some extent, but, depending on that extent, unnecessary and even tragic problems can be put in place, which may or may not be resolved later in life.

Empathy for and with the preverbal child is crucially important, and is equally important as she finds the words to express her needs and preferences. Time and patience given to understand her point of view, even if you cannot agree with her, will pay enormous dividends into your relationship with your child and into your child's emotional health bank.

There is so much that we can learn from the client/counsellor relationship that would help us understand what it is to be a child in a world full of adults and so enrich our parent/child relationships and all our child/adult relationships. Most importantly the counsellor can provide what was unavailable in early relationships. Key words in the relationship with the counsellor are: trust, closeness, intimacy, flexibility, encouragement, warmth, safety, mutuality, caring, compassion, kindness. These are words parents can incorporate into their relationships with their children as well.

Above all, the relationship between client and counsellor is a *benign* one, and our relationship with our child needs to be benign too. If it isn't, we need to ask ourselves what is it in ourselves that is getting in the way of this most important of all relationships. Being valued by the counsellor enables a client to gradually value themselves. But why did they have to wait to be valued by a counsellor?

One of the key qualities that Carl Rogers identified as being vital to a therapeutic relationship was congruence on the part of the counsellor. Congruence means genuineness, being who we are, self-acceptance. We achieve this state – one in which we don't have to score points at the expense of another person, particularly a vulnerable child – by being self-aware. That is, being aware of what motivates us. Self-awareness is crucially important not only for our relationship with our child but for all our relationships and so it becomes the subject of another chapter.

HOW COUNSELLING THEORY CAN ENRICH OUR PARENTING – SUMMARIES

◆ How we should all emerge from childhood.
◆ The quality of the client/counsellor relationship is integral to the healing process.
◆ The client needs a safe containing space as do children.
◆ Neither counsellors nor parents have to be all-powerful or always right.
◆ To a degree we are all composed of a 'true self' and a 'false self'.
◆ A midlife crisis is an important opportunity for growth.
◆ Counselling seeks to provide the right atmosphere.
◆ The right atmosphere empowers the 'true self'.
◆ How honest can a child be with parents, carers and teachers about what may be troubling them?
◆ How to create the right atmosphere.
◆ The empathic response of the counsellor is a healing response.
◆ The importance of being self-aware so that unhelpful cycles don't get passed from one generation to another.

2

EDUCATION FOR LIFE
The Theories

'The single most important contribution education can make to a child's development is to help him toward a field where his talents best suit him, where he will be satisfied and competent. We've completely lost sight of that. Instead we subject everyone to an education where, if you succeed, you will be best suited to be a college professor. And we evaluate everyone along the way according to whether they meet that narrow standard of success. We should spend less time ranking children and more time helping them to identify their natural competencies and gifts; and cultivate those. There are hundreds and hundreds of ways to succeed, and many, many different abilities that will help you get there.'

Howard Gardner

'Adler, during the last twenty years of his life, had emphasised the need to educate teachers, who have influence over large numbers of children, so that the ideas of Individual Psychology could benefit future generations and prevent mental illness. Dreikurs too concentrated his efforts on

teaching parents and teachers so that children could be enabled to grow up mentally healthy and psychologically able to participate in a democratic society.'

Jenny Warner

One sentiment I heard repeatedly expressed with great feeling during the years of my counselling training, and which I whole-heartedly agreed with, was, 'I wish I'd known all this before I had my children.' But how could we, unless we had been fortunate enough to have had it included in the curriculum at school? What makes our counselling training so important is that, by its very nature, it engenders a greater understanding of ourselves and others. In our multicultural society this is probably more important today than it has ever been. But the main reason for includ-ing it in the curriculum would be to give teenagers an insight into why they feel the way they do about themselves and certain issues, as well as insights that would help them to understand and perhaps tolerate others more readily. All of which could be of tremendous value to young people as they step out into the world.

By looking briefly at what certain therapeutic approaches have to offer, I hope to show just how much could be learnt from them, if this knowledge was widely available. We need it, most of all, before we embark on the most important task of our lives, namely that of enabling the next generation to grow up, as Dreikurs advo-cated, 'mentally healthy and psychologically able to participate in a democratic society'. In other words, to grow up happy, balanced and able to fulfil their unique potential.

PSYCHODYNAMIC THEORY

So let us start with psychodynamic theory which grew out of Freud's basic premise, that the content of the unconscious influences our conscious thoughts, emotions and actions. This being the case, it is crucially important to become aware of where those unconscious influences originated and how they impact on our daily life.

Freud claimed that, up to the age of six, harmful experiences would be repressed, but that their effects would continue to affect an individual throughout their life. He said that we 'bury things alive', pushing them out of conscious awareness, where, ostensibly forgotten, they nevertheless continue to exert a powerful influence. Because of this, psychic energy is tied up in 'forgetting' rather than being available to enable us to live more fully in the present. So for healing to take place, the experience would, in some way, have to be confronted and worked through.

When a client makes a link between something which is troubling them in their life now and something they experienced in the past, that link is an important breakthrough, a catalyst for healing. There is a good example of this in Chapter 12, so for now all I will add is that acknowledging an experience and its lingering impact goes a long way towards lessening that impact and over time it can even eradicate it completely. It is an interesting theory, which makes us aware of how important it is to find out why we act or react in certain ways.

'AS IF' APPROACH

Alfred Adler also believed that the early years were important. During these early years we form a basic conception of ourselves, imbibed from parents and siblings, which results in our own 'private logic' which in turn shapes our lives. This 'private logic' – how we see ourselves received in the world – is crucially important. It influences the two innate drives that Adler believed we have, one to *belong*, the other to *overcome* our dependence on others. It is quite a delicate balancing act because as little children we need to know and experience a safe and secure dependency before we can be safely and securely independent. If we postulate a 'self-fulfilling prophecy' for each of us as Adler did (that what we expect from ourselves and from others will turn out to be true), then the implications of that private logic assume enormous proportions. Will it help or hinder the three major life-tasks that he believed confronted us all, namely occupation, friendship and love?

Adler was essentially an optimist urging an 'as if' approach to life. It was important to have a goal and to project into the future. What he was doing was giving us permission to aspire. Permission that we might not have received from anywhere else. Permission to achieve, rather than being stopped in our tracks by a sense of failure, by the limitations that other people put on us. Such a process, leading to a goal, emphasises that we don't have to be stuck in the past, limited by unhelpful patterns of thought and behaviour.

PERSON-CENTRED COUNSELLING

In Person-Centred counselling, a therapy developed by the psychiatrist Carl Rogers, the importance of respect for ourselves and for others is the key concept. He wanted his theory to benefit all aspects of life which of course is exactly what respect does. Fundamental to his person-centred work was the belief that at some level the client knows what is hurting, and that the empathic engagement of the counsellor will help them articulate this and begin the work of healing. This was quite an innovative approach for its time.

Carl Rogers believed in the importance of really 'listening' to what was being said. In addition to this, his therapy emerged as a result of his strongly held beliefs in human nature. That is to say that he saw each person as unique and believed in the fundamental *goodness* of human nature and the essential trustworthiness to be found in each person. He believed that people have a potential for growth, which, even when deeply buried, can be breathed into life again, by many things, including therapy.

This is an approach which allows for the subjective reality of the client (how the world appears to them), what they are thinking, feeling and experiencing. Acknowledging and nurturing this inner world strengthens inner resources. For a teenager, as for an adult, learning how important recognition of their inner world is, could give them an appreciation and understanding of themselves not previously experienced.

Rogers believed that everyone had within them the potential for change and growth. He called this potential the 'mainspring of life'. In counselling, the task for the counsellor is to create an *atmosphere* where this mainspring, this self-actualisation of the client, can take place. But where this sadly has not been the case, learning about it as a reality within, could be the first step towards getting in touch with it and enjoying a more meaningful life.

What cannot be stressed enough is how important the attitude of others is towards us, especially in the early years. As young children and as adolescents, we are literally built or broken on the altar of other people's attitudes towards us. Rogers endorsed this when he wrote that studies have shown that attitudes can be 'growth promoting' or 'growth inhibiting'. He emphasises that the most important and helpful attitude for nurturing healthy growth is quite simply 'acceptance'.

This finding was endorsed by clients who stressed that they felt that it was the attitude of the counsellor towards them that allowed for changes to take place in their lives. They stressed the importance of being listened to properly, having someone's undivided attention, the ensuing trust, and the feeling of being understood. All these contributed to a sense of independence and with that independence came the confidence to own feelings and make decisions. In short and importantly for the individual, there can be a meaningful shift away from disempowering feelings of self-doubt and inadequacy and a feeling that they always have to take their cue from what others say or want. To a self that allows for a growing sense of awareness, a valuing of who they are and of being in charge of their own life. A gradual move from the self-doubt which is so crippling, to the beginnings of autonomy.

Surely no one can doubt the value of this. Rogers himself said that he had found a way of working with clients that had 'much constructive potential'. He also gave us a philosophy of life and interaction with the world that provides a foundation of immeasurable value to all of us but one that is especially important for young people . A foundation that can facilitate meaningful contacts and interactions, in all areas of life.

SELF-AWARENESS

Just a brief look at these therapies illustrates the common thread that runs through them: the need for self-awareness. Why we act in the way we do and why we respond in the way we do. Are these actions and responses what we want or are they habitual and in need of changing? It also gives some insights as to what may be gained by finding a way to include these therapies in our children's education.

TRANSACTIONAL ANALYSIS

Transactional Analysis was introduced by Eric Berne in an attempt to release people from negative influences. Berne believed that we all start out as princes and princesses but that negative influences and experiences turn us into frogs. In order for us to get back to who we could and should be, we have to free ourselves from these influences and we do this by becoming aware of how we act in certain situations. Dividing our personality into child, parent and adult, we needed to become aware of which part of ourselves is triggered in certain situations. So, for instance, we might find that someone is acting like an authoritative parent and our child might be triggered, thus putting us at a distinct disadvantage. Being aware of these different parts of our personality could help us counteract any negative impact.

GESTALT THERAPY

Another interesting therapy which can help throw light on our interactions with others is Gestalt Therapy. This therapy was developed by Fritz Perls who advocated living in the here and now and taking responsibility for our own lives. Also an important part of his therapy is the *empty chair method* whereby a client sits opposite an empty chair. The client then imagines someone sitting in that chair who has wronged them and they tell them just how they feel. (Remember the person isn't there so no harm can be done.) Then they go and sit in the empty chair and imagine they are that person and what it was like for that person to be told those things. It is possible that the client would come to understand the other person's perspective and so begin the work of healing.

BEHAVIOURAL AND COGNITIVE THERAPIES

More recent therapies are Behavioural and Cognitive therapy. Behavioural therapy believes that all behaviour is learned behaviour, so it follows that with the right guidance anything unhelpful or harmful can be unlearned. Cognitive therapy focuses on how our thoughts can influence our moods and actions for better or worse. All of which allow a deeper understanding of how we 'work' and we can use that understanding to bring about change and healing where it's needed.

TRANSPERSONAL PSYCHOLOGY

Transpersonal Psychology acknowledges our spiritual potential and seeks the health of the whole person, so like Maslow's hierarchy of needs it embraces our wholeness. Even looking at Erikson's stages of growth, from birth right through to old age, would give an insight into the different tasks that confront us from infancy to old age, and I'm sure such insights would by their very nature be a catalyst for self-awareness and engender respect for the life experience of self and others.

Youngsters introduced to these ideas would gain insights into their own complexity and richness and the complexity and richness of others. If we found room for this in our children's education, we would be finding room to teach them about their human being-ness. We would be offering something interesting, enduring and hopeful to them, on the threshold of adult life. Something that, sooner rather than later, would provide them with more effective tools and skills to cope with and enjoy life.

As yet, our society fails to teach and so acknowledge and open up to children the world they carry within themselves, with its vast riches and potential. It is possible that teaching children about different counselling theories could help to change that.

EDUCATION FOR LIFE – SUMMARIES

◆ Counselling training engenders a greater understanding of ourselves and others.

◆ How unconscious influences originate and how they impact our lives.

◆ 'Forgotten' experiences can continue to exert a powerful influence.

◆ We need to know why we act or react in certain ways.

◆ Our 'private logic' about ourselves, imbibed from others, shapes our lives for better or worse.

◆ Children must experience a secure dependency before they can be safely and securely independent.

◆ Adler postulated three major life tasks: occupation, friendship and love.

◆ The importance of respect for self and others.

◆ Rogers believed in the fundamental goodness of human nature.

◆ The crucial importance of other people's attitude towards us especially in childhood.

◆ What different therapies can contribute to our understanding.

◆ Attitudes can be 'growth promoting' or 'growth inhibiting'.

◆ The most important and helpful attitude is simply 'acceptance'.

◆ The importance of acknowledging the child's inner world.

3

THE SIMPLE NEEDS
OF THE BABY

'Two things are necessary if the emotional centre is to grow and become available and present in our interactions with others: the infant must feel loved by his mother first and foremost, then by his father and other family members close to him; and his own love must be received in a similar way. The fundamental trauma for the child is either that he or she is not loved or that his or her love is not received.'

Neville Symington

'Julie wanted very much to have a child. When Wendy was born, Julie was generous with her milk, her holding and stroking, and her other ways of caring. These gifts helped Wendy grow and blossom, and she felt good about herself and her world from the very start...

Deborah thought she wanted a child, but really didn't. She was always busy with other things, even after Ginny was born. Ginny often didn't get enough to eat, or enough love and caring. She sensed her mother's coldness and within the first few months of life, developed a "basic mistrust": "Life is hostile; the struggle isn't worth it, because basically I won't get what I want (need)." Many years later, Ginny is still haunted by a nagging fear that she "won't get enough."'

Daniels and Horowitz

'...at the beginning of our lives, each of us was born into this world a tiny, yet magnificent baby with limitless potential and a beautiful heart. And that beautiful newborn heart wanted nothing more than to love and be loved.'

Fred Burks

These extracts confirm the simple truth that, above all, what a baby needs is to be wanted and loved. To be welcome in the world. The baby needs someone – mother, father, carer – to be 'preoccupied' by their presence in the world and to be prepared to put, as far as possible, all unnecessary activities 'on hold' for the foreseeable future.

No child has asked to be born, so to be wanted and loved should be the unquestioned birthright of every child. That is to say, every baby should be entitled to a simple caring love, such as Julie was able to make available to Wendy in the Daniels and Horowitz quote above.

W. D. Winnicott stressed that the 'ordinary' things that we do for a baby are important and constitute the foundations of a healthy emotional life. And the importance of these 'ordinary things' was endorsed by psychologist Erik Erikson's theory, which postulates eight stages of development that each of us negotiates during our lifetime. In the first year he stressed the importance of the baby being able to develop trust as opposed to mistrust. Trust nurtured by safe containment, with needs being met, allowing for a secure dependency and safe attachment, which is the foundation of a secure independence.

We can see the difference this can make from the opening quotes about Wendy and Ginny. The simple caring love that Wendy received will foster trust in life, while the distractions of Ginny's mother leave Ginny with a deficit, which may or may not find healing through friendship, counselling or a loving relationship. I would say that, for the majority of clients I have worked with, trust is the basic issue that needs to be addressed. Winnicott says that one way to nurture trust is through patience; patience which allows for the playfulness of the baby to express itself. It is precisely this playfulness which provides the clue to the beginnings of a unique inner life in the baby which flourishes with the responsiveness of the parent.

That's quite a thought isn't it: that the playfulness of our baby is testament to the fact that *already present in this tiny being is an inner life, a mind that is reaching out to engage with us*? An inner life, which is shaped and impacted by our responses to it. And our responses, for better or worse, become the crucial foundation for our baby's life, throughout infancy, childhood, adolescence and adulthood.

Strategies for patience:

- Perhaps the most important thing we can do is to relax. It's much easier to be patient in a relaxed state.
- Looking after your own emotional well-being will allow you to have some reserves and help you to be available to your baby.

- Stay calm.
- The will to good and kindness will nurture the flow of love for both of you.
- Some simple meditation or mindfulness techniques can help foster patience.
- You may find Izzy Judd's *Mindfulness for Mums* helpful, especially the exercise 'Calm begins with me'.
- Not all of us find it easy to be patient but we can learn to be patient and it will pay dividends with the evolving little person's emotional and mental health bank.

A FOUNDATION OF LOVE

Edward Carpenter, an eighteenth century philosopher, said that throughout the body of the infant there is 'an intelligence seeking to find expression'. We only have to look at a baby to know that this is true. Every glance, every movement is an intelligence seeking to find expression, seeking to understand and to be understood. And what Edward Carpenter said would have been perfectly understood by Dr. Ian Suttie. In his book, *Origins of Love and Hate*, he draws on twenty-five years of work with mothers and babies, to stress the importance of early relationships, particularly between the baby and mother and the mutuality which he found in their relationship.

That is to say that it isn't a one-sided relationship. The mother and father gain something of immense importance from the relationship with their baby. Although if their hearts are closed to what the baby brings them, or if there are simply too many distractions, they put at risk the most precious relationship of their life.

He believed that an understanding of the origins of love and hate would provide insights into our human nature as individuals and into society as a whole. To understand the need for love and the many ways in which its absence allows for destructive emotions to take hold, such as frustration, depression, humiliation, despair, anger, hate and violence, would be to begin the work of healing ourselves and our communities. His observations convinced him that the early love we receive provides each of us with a stable foundation from which we can go out and meet the world.

A CARING RESPONSE

As babies, we are born in a state of total dependency and possess what Dr. Suttie describes as an 'innate need-for-companionship'. Put simply, this innate need is for self-preservation, for survival, and should engender a loving or, at the very least, a caring response. Sadly, there are times when a baby's innate impulse is not enough to unlock a wounded, harsh or defended heart. When this happens the baby's present and future life is compromised, and a child brought up by a parent or parents where, for whatever reason, there is an absence of love, no 'connection', will be emotionally handicapped. There is nothing to show for it on the outside, just as with a depressed person there is no obvious wound. Clients have said to me that because they haven't got anything to *show* for the way they are feeling, no broken bones, no allowances are made for the struggle and pain that are going on inside them. The same applies to the child in a loveless childhood. And the truth will probably not even be acknowledged when, for some, this struggle and pain emerge as an eating disorder or violence or sometimes, tragically, suicide.

It cannot be stressed enough, that *this isn't about blame*. It's about being absolutely honest about what we would do differently if only we could, so that those who would like to can learn from our mistakes.

Dr. Suttie stresses the importance of this early love by saying that a baby's present and future psychological health and sense of security (that's yours and mine) has its beginnings in, and is dependent on, the reciprocal, social, love relationship that is experienced with the primary care-giver.

FEELINGS ARE ALL BABIES HAVE

What is crucially important about all of this is how we are made to *feel*. After all, before birth, during birth, after birth and during the preverbal phase, all we have – *all we have* – are our feelings. These feelings tell us (communicate to us), in the deepest fabric of our being, what sort of world, what sort of environment, we have been born into. And this message is a very powerful one which will stay with each one of us for the rest of our life. So what did the doctors, nurses and parents – the hands that first touched us – what did they communicate to us?

The importance of this is so powerfully illustrated by the circumstances of the birth of the great ballet dancer Rudolf Nureyev. Writing about his life, Julie Kavanagh tells us that he was born as his mother travelled on a Trans-Siberian train. His birth was greeted by her joy at the birth of a longed-for son and the rhythmic sound of the train and these two early influences had an enduring effect. We are told that as a boy in ballet school he would climb the hill above where he lived to watch and listen to the trains below. As a dancer with the Kirov Ballet Company, when he wanted inspiration to create a new role, he would sit in Leningrad station watching the trains until he and the movement and rhythm of the trains became one. So the circumstances of his birth made a fundamental contribution to a brilliant career and we should never underestimate the impact of the circumstances of our birth on the rest of our life.

Everything tells us that the nurture of the infant has far-reaching implications and is concerned with far more than merely the satisfying of bodily needs. We learn from a very early age what to expect from those around us and, by extension, from the world as a whole. This is a message that influences the rest of our life. It is a simple yet delicately balanced process, which inevitably courts anxiety and frustration for both the infant and the mother. Even so, Dr. Suttie emphasises the infant's right to make 'angry claims' on parents whose caring falls short of meeting the infant's *instinctual* need for self-preservation, whether physical, psychological or emotional. What a baby needs, he says, is to feel personally cared for and wanted. Quite simply it is affection, tenderness and love (a 'mental sympathy' providing care, compassion and common sense) which provide our 'base supplies' for life.

All of the above not only reinforces the importance of the attitude of the parents to their baby but the fact that the baby contributes in a meaningful way to the relationship. This awareness of the baby's contribution to the relationship with its parents, formed the basis of the work of Berry Brazelton. His experience as a paediatrician, trained in child psychiatry, showed him that a newborn baby, far from being passive, was in fact able to recognise its mother's face, voice and smell. Interestingly and importantly, the baby's behaviour is acknowledged to be its 'language' and at the very least we should try to understand this tiny person's attempts to communicate in this vast incomprehensible world. Brazelton also endorses what Dr. Suttie says regarding the fact that a baby is an individual with abilities already present. Above all, he reminds us of the baby's contribution to the relationship with its parents.

Strategies for responding to baby's angry claims:

- First of all let us consider: are they 'angry claims' or might they be 'just claims'?
- If we think of them as 'just claims', it may help us to see them as claims we would ourselves be entitled to make given similar circumstances.
- After all, this little person didn't ask to be born.
- So perhaps we can take Julia Cameron's 'affectionate listening' and make it 'affectionate responding'.
- Remember: however tired we are, our response is shaping a life.
- Compassion for the needs of the baby in our care will help us to be what this baby needs from us: tender, responsive, containing.
- Also, looking after our own needs as much as possible will allow us some reserves to meet the instinctual needs of our baby.

WHAT WE CARRY IN OUR BODIES

So we can say that the needs of a baby can be comfortably met for parent and baby with simplicity, compassion and kindness, where love for whatever reason isn't possible. But before we move on, there is just one further thought I would like to leave with you. I believe that we are born communicating at a psychic level. The Chinese Taoist tradition acknowledges this when it says 'The new born child is still connected to the Tao, to the source of its life and its arising.' [4] That is to say, our mind is joined to all of life, and to those around us, as it was with the mother who carried us. And perhaps the baby's first task in life is to make a transition from this state of oneness to a place of communication with the world through each of the five senses. Not an easy task.

I have often had clients say to me that babies don't understand anything. This is particularly true of people in destructive relationships, who don't want to admit to themselves that the atmosphere that they are creating may have a detrimental effect on their baby. Understandably they don't like it when I say that the baby is like a sponge, and she soaks up everything. What I also believe (but don't say) is that everything we experience is recorded at some level in our body. Nothing is really forgotten. Take an elderly person with dementia, seemingly out of touch with the present and recent past; they can remember long forgotten dates and events: it is all still *there* somewhere. It is simply a question of a certain button being pressed to access the memory. In just the same way, long forgotten events can be triggered by circumstances at any time in our lives. We take on board our mother's feelings (especially for us) and the feelings of those around us and it can take a very long time in later life to sort out where such feelings are coming from. I know we are making an enormous leap from the simple needs of the baby to how that baby's life will play out in adolescence and adulthood, but the fact remains that seeds sown in infancy can have repercussions in later life.

THE SIMPLE NEEDS OF THE BABY – SUMMARIES

◆ To be wanted and loved should be the birthright of every child.

◆ The ordinary things you do for your baby provide the foundations for a healthy emotional life.

◆ Safe containment allows trust to develop.

◆ Trust makes possible a secure dependency which later makes possible a secure independence.

◆ The baby's playfulness is proof of an inner life reaching out to engage with us.

◆ Dr. Suttie stresses the importance of recognising the mutuality of the relationship with your baby.

◆ The absence of love or even simple kindness allows for the possibility of destructive emotions taking hold.

◆ Simple care, compassion and common sense can provide the baby's 'base supplies' for life.

◆ Everything a baby knows is mediated through feelings; feelings that will stay with them throughout their life.

4

THE TERRIFIC TWOS

'...you can behave as you think you should, but without entirely wanting to do so. This produces consistent behaviour, but entails great strain...the mind and the behaviour are out of accord, resulting in a situation in which you are doing what you do not wholly want to do. This arouses a sense of coercion that usually produces rage...'

A Course In Miracles

'The body is a network of messages constantly being transmitted and received. Some of these messages nourish and sustain us, while others lead to disorder and breakdown.'

Deepak Chopra

I often hear people refer to the 'terrible twos' and always wonder just who it is most 'terrible' for, the carer or the infant? A woman once told me that her grandson had reached the terrible twos stage early. She said he was into everything and what a lot of trouble he was for his mother and her. He was obviously a loved child but, nevertheless, 'he' was the problem.

I asked her if she had ever thought what life might be like for him? Up until now he had spent all his life at the mercy of his bodily needs and functions. He had known the awful pain of hunger. He'd been wet and cold. He'd been lonely and afraid. He had cried and no one had come. He'd been given plain biscuits when he'd have liked chocolate ones (wouldn't we all?). He'd been put in bath water that was too hot or too cold. He'd been made to drink stuff he didn't like. He had made sounds that no one had understood. He had been laughed at, and somehow the laughter had hurt him. Now at last he had reached a place where he could understand and imitate a few of the sounds that seemed to make sense to the people around him. He could let them know what he was feeling. He could let them know what his preferences where. And what happened most of the time? Most of the time, his precious, infant, individuating self was being overruled. Sometimes of course for the best possible reason, but often simply to conform to an adult agenda that didn't seem to take account of him. How would we, as adults, respond to such treatment?

This, or at least something close to it, was what I said, and the woman walked off with her nose in the air, clearly put out. Why? Because I hadn't colluded with her and her daughter, as we in the adult world are supposed to do. We are supposed to sympathise with how difficult it is to be a parent. *Which of course it is.* But some of us remember just how difficult it is to be a child, in a world where people seemed to have forgotten, just how difficult it is to be a child, in a world full of adults who have forgotten…

THE ADULT WITHIN THE CHILD

Not only do adults forget how difficult and confusing the adult world can be to a child, they forget too, that the child will one day be an adult, and that how that adult life fulfils itself is, to a great extent, dependent on what they themselves are doing with the child at this very moment in time. Just how much an adult can forget that the baby will one day be an adult was brought home to me by a conversation I had with a health visitor and a midwife. The health visitor asked the midwife how she responded to a baby who didn't like being bathed. The midwife said that she just continued. The health visitor said that it was possible that the baby might grow into an adult with a fear of water. To which the midwife replied that, in all her thirty years delivering babies, she had only seen them as 'babies', not as potential adults.

So not being able to see the adult in the infant or child is not as unlikely as we might think. How many of us are aware that our child's adult, that is the adult they will one day be, hears and sees everything we say and do to our child? The adult in the child is a witness to everything we say and do. This inability to see the adult in the child is touched on by Winnicott in his book *The Family and Individual Development*. He describes how a mother's intuitive response to her baby's disability is overruled by hospital staff. The proposed treatment would restrict the use of the baby's arm and the mother was aware that her baby had reached the stage in her development where she instinctively wanted to reach out and touch the objects around her. She was concerned about the long-term emotional impact of anything interfering with this instinctive attempt by her baby to interact with her world. Winnicott's point was that, while undoubtedly well meaning, what he called the physically-minded specialists couldn't see beyond the baby, to the adult she would one day become and the possible wider implications of the treatment they were proposing.

Another incident which brought home to me how we can so easily misunderstand a young child was during a conversation I had with another health visitor. She was telling me about a little girl of two. Her mother had recently had another baby and the health visitor remarked that when the mother fed the new baby the little girl wanted to breastfeed too, because she could smell the milk. The health visitor said of the little girl, 'She's greedy.' But I couldn't help wondering about that little girl. Was she greedy? Or did the smell of her mother's milk, and the closeness of the mother and baby, remind her of a time when life was simpler, less confusing and more comfortable? And was there something in her that longed to return to that cosy place, if only for a moment?

AUTONOMY

For Erikson, this is the second stage of our development, from one to three years, and the task is identified as autonomy versus shame and doubt. Where a young child is encouraged and praised for his achievements, the foundations of confidence and a secure sense of self are laid. Where however his efforts are discouraged or belittled, or where he is expected to do more than it is reasonable to expect of him, the seeds of doubt and shame are sown. Again, many clients who come into counselling need to regain a sense of autonomy and overcome feelings of self-doubt and shame. All of which is avoidable.

If we just stop and think about what is achieved in the first few years we can only be amazed. Let us really be prepared to reflect on what happens. The process of giving birth can be an agonising one for the mother. Contractions are often violent, relentless and painful. If it is painful for the mother, it is probably fair to assume that the experience is painful for the baby too: something over which a baby has no control and which they cannot decide to opt out of. After birth everything must be experienced as an assault on their delicate nervous system. I remember reading that very premature babies cannot be touched. Even the tender touch of a loving parent can be too much for their immature nervous system.

During the first months, we undertake a bewildering transition into the world of the senses. If there are congenital problems, this first stage can be as difficult as it is important. Even where there are no physiological problems containment and gentleness are paramount. It is really self-evident that problems encountered at this early stage, whether physiological, emotional and/or environmental, will be deeply rooted, fundamental problems.

Sensory perception gradually becomes conscious perception. That is to say, sensations come to have meaning and causes. It will be a time of excitement and alarm and it is so important to try to understand what the experience of being in the world is like for the infant child, and to respond compassionately to this experience. At this stage the infant will have begun to make sense of the sounds around him. He may even be making his first coherent communications. And do we ever stop to wonder at this miracle? While so much is going on for the toddler at a developmental and emotional level, he is actually learning a language.

Anyone who has tried to learn a foreign language (unless they are particularly gifted) knows how difficult it is to make themselves understood in the early attempts. Yet we have our own language to fall back on, to explain what we are trying to say. The infant doesn't have this. As for so much else in a toddler's experience, the whole exercise is one of trial and error and, at the last, it is an enormous achievement, which can so easily be taken for granted.

We dismiss the enormity of the tasks being undertaken by the evolving little person, by calling this period *the terrible twos* when in fact we should be calling it *the terrific twos* in acknowledgement of the enormity of the tasks achieved, sometimes under the most difficult of circumstances.

Each stage flows into another with an oscillating motion; nothing is fixed. But what will get 'fixed' are the problems arising from this stage, because parents or carers either don't appreciate the enormous tasks that confront each infant, or aren't prepared to take them into consideration when interacting with them. And there is a particular task which faces each of us, equally as important as walking or talking, and which, in fact, has enormous implications for the whole of our lives. And that task is *learning how to express our emotions in a way that is both acceptable to parents and society and wholesome for our evolving self.*

What we *feel* is who we are. How those who care for us respond to our feelings affects our sense of self, and dictates how safe it is for us to be that self. Or how much of a 'false self' will have to take control or our lives.

AFFECTIONATE LISTENING

Now, when I see a child having a tantrum, I want to say to the parents, 'He is trying to tell you something. You must do better than reduce him to this.' And surely our children deserve that we make the effort to understand what's happening for them? Especially if you consider that a tantrum is all that a child has left by way of communication, to let you know that he desperately needs to be heard and seen, and to have his feelings taken into consideration.

So often the trauma of a tantrum could be avoided for the toddler as well as the parent if the parent or carer could just take a step back and think about what's happening. After all, we are the adult, we brought this little person into the world or undertook to care for them, depending on the circumstances. Compassion should move us to do our best, to understand them and respond helpfully. So if you think your child is being naughty, perhaps approaching a tantrum, think again.

Perhaps you need to listen, and when I say listen, Julia Cameron's *affectionate listening* comes to mind. Just thinking those words can have a magical effect on how we might respond to someone, and our response to a child is as important as a counsellor's response to what a client brings to a session. This response is crucially important because it can make the difference between the work of healing or compounding the damage already caused. Carl Rogers' Person-Centred therapy and his core conditions also come to mind here. In *On Becoming A Person* he explains that it is the warmth and understanding the client finds within the relationship with the counsellor that allows him to understand what is going on inside himself. And we can extend that warmth, that affectionate listening, to ourselves as well as our child – so not only listen to your child but to yourself. Are you projecting your adult interpretation onto your child? It could be, and usually is, a very different perspective.

We need to think about how we might have contributed to the situation. Have we been misunderstood? Is clearer communication needed? Consideration and respect are necessary. In short, we should *want* to defuse the situation, not add to it. A friend told me that her daughter did exactly this when her little son was working himself up into a tantrum. She stopped in her tracks and just asked herself what was happening for him and for herself. In doing this, she realised that it was her stress he was picking up on and that she had projected her feelings onto what he was doing. He wasn't the cause but he was in danger of taking the fallout from the way she was feeling.

I said to her that I thought it was wonderful that her daughter had cared enough to do that and been honest enough to admit to herself that the problem had originated with her. That her innocent little boy was in danger of taking the blame for what she was feeling, just as I know my children did in the early years when I could so easily be overwhelmed by the feelings of past and present emotions. I think this happens more often than we might like to admit. We aren't feeling good or we are worrying about something and have allowed ourselves to get into a negative state so that our child's behaviour grates with us. If we hadn't been in that negative place their behaviour, even if it had been something we didn't like, would almost certainly have been addressed in a different way.

Strategies to use if a tantrum seems imminent:

- ◆ Take a step back and do your best to let go of your anger and/or frustration.
- ◆ Be honest with yourself about your contribution to the situation.
- ◆ This will help you to find the empathy to put your feelings to one side, feelings which might otherwise exacerbate the situation.

- What is happening to and inside the toddler?
- Is what the toddler wants/needs really so unreasonable?
- Try to understand their perspective; what's happening for them?
- Compassion and kindness can help you make your child's well-being your ultimate priority. Neither of you need this distress, so preventing the situation from escalating is in both your interests.
- As adults we should be able to turn the situation around.

INDEPENDENCE

In everything that's going on for our child and for ourselves, we need to remember that the developing child has to cope with the conflict of learning self-assertion, which is linked to confidence, and also learning to fit in with others. When this aspect of a child's development meets with co-operation and compromise from those around him, the outcome for the child is good. Where, on the other hand, a child meets with intolerance, the result is a loss of the self or a frustrated, rebellious child. It isn't always easy but to respond to our child with understanding, or at least with the *wish* to understand, is to teach co-operation, which he in turn can emulate. With this approach, daily life and the individuation of ourselves (because we never finish this task) and the individuation of our child, become a mutual endeavour. Michael Jacobs, writing in *The Presenting Past*, says that tantrums or rebelliousness are a natural part of development and can manifest at any point in the life of an individual. From babyhood to old age there is a need for a delicate balance between safe containment and the freedom to express and experience the fulfilment of individual needs and wishes, whether they are physical, emotional or psychological. So much depends on the carer being able to stand gentle but firm when it is vitally important that they do so, while also knowing when compassion for the intrinsic well-being of the other, whatever their age, requires a different response.

So, if your child is having a tantrum you need to stop and ask yourself what is happening and be very sure of how you handle the situation, regardless of how tired you are or how unreasonable you think your child is being. Often, when we do stop to think, it is ourselves who have misunderstood our child, or not made ourselves clear. If you don't stop to consider this, unsympathetic treatment at this time in a child's development can result in what is known as a fragmented self. That is a weak, vulnerable self, beholden to everyone, rather than a strong and stable sense of self. Sadly, having a fragmented, weak self can eventually result in the person having distressing symptoms of which the list is endless and uncomfortable and, above all, avoidable. Remember these conditions don't come from nowhere. Babies are not born with them. They can arise because an infant or child has been put through experiences that they just could not cope with. As it says in that opening quote from *A Course in Miracles*, coercion produces rage, and we know, from the rage that so quickly surfaces when some people get behind the wheel of a car, just how much rage is stored in people from their past, from trying to fit into a role imposed by someone else.

All of this illustrates how crucial the early years are if we are to enjoy fulfilling relationships throughout our lives. Also, if we accept that in counselling the most important qualities we can bring to our work with clients are empathy -that is putting our feelings to one side and being aware of our client's perspective, what they are experiencing in this moment – and; compassion; being non-judgemental, accepting and kind; and, most importantly, having the well-being of the client as our priority; then these must be the simple but necessary qualities needed in every parent and carer to prevent these feelings taking root in the first place or, if they have taken root while our back was turned, be the means by which we can restore calm.

It can be very difficult to be little in a world full of adults. Doris Lessing, in her book *Memoirs of a Survivor*, hauntingly evokes the world of dependence. She clearly shows that she understands and maybe remembers what it is like to be two and have your needs or actions misinterpreted as we adults can often do, preoccupied as we are with problems or seeing something from an adult rather than an infant perspective. What she actually writes doesn't make easy reading. But what she says is so important because she illustrates vividly and painfully how the cycle of unkindness can be passed from generation to generation. Only our awareness of how we could and should be, of what the infant and evolving child needs for holistic, healthy development, will help us undo the harmful effects of these destructive and tragic cycles.

OLDER SIBLINGS

I would just like to add one more very important thought here which is that it is very often when a child is around the terrific twos that another baby comes on the scene. This can happen when the toddler is still a 'baby', still developing in so many important and complex ways: physically, psychologically and emotionally; still very much in need of the care, love and affection which can be experienced as being taken away from them and going to the new baby brother or sister.

I remember hearing a mother speaking on the radio. She said that when her little boy was born her daughter (who was by then two) seemed so big compared to the tiny baby, who was so dependent on her, that she expected the little girl to do more for herself than was reasonable. Looking back she deeply regretted the way she treated her because of this perception. It's important to bear in mind that the older toddler is still in need of consideration and tender loving care.

Strategy: When the Older Child Wants to Join In

- Such feelings can easily be mitigated by allowing the sibling to help in small ways.
- Be careful though, to only ask them to help within their capabilities.
- Really appreciate what they do by praising them for their helpfulness.
- In this way you will allow them to feel included and valued.
- Importantly you are not only nurturing their self-esteem but also nurturing the sibling and family bonds.

To feel understood and appreciated is important all through life, but most especially as a foundation in the formative years. In a wonderfully insightful poem, 'Children Learn What They Live', the late Dorothy Law Nolte reminds us how debilitating negative influences are, and how important positive responses and reinforcements are for healthy development. Amongst the qualities she cites as being important are encouragement, tolerance, praise, acceptance, approval and honesty, all of which empower children to give and receive love and to feel secure in the world.

THE TERRIFIC TWOS – SUMMARIES

◆ How hard it is to be a child in a world where adults have forgotten what it is to be a child in a world where adults have forgotten....

◆ The child will one day be an adult and how that life fulfils itself depends to a great extent on the care they've received.

◆ The adult in the child hears and see everything we do. Nothing is forgotten.

◆ The task at this stage is autonomy versus shame and doubt. Autonomy is life affirming, shame is crippling.

◆ With everything the toddler is doing at this stage they are also learning a language with nothing to fall back on but our responses to his/her efforts, hence 'Terrific Twos'.

◆ Learning to express those all-important emotions is about finding a balance between what is acceptable to parents and society and what is wholesome for our evolving self.

◆ See a tantrum as the toddler's communication of last resort.

◆ When a second or third child comes along don't forget the older child or children. It's a big ask but it will pay dividends beyond imagination in the future for you and your child.

5

THE MATERNAL INSTINCT

'The mother is everything in life. She is the consolation in our sadness, the hope in our distress, the strength in our weakness. She is the source of compassion, she is love and grace.'

Kahlil Gibran

Where the maternal instinct is alive and well, Gibran's description is not as idealistic as we might think. It is, after all, probably the most important quality that anyone will ever experience from another person or in themselves. I remember one writer who described it as the human quality that would eventually save the world. It is the nurturing energy a mother makes available to her child, which makes possible balanced, happy growth. And it isn't really difficult to do this if Winnicott is right when he says, 'In the ordinary things you do you are quite naturally doing very important things.' [2]

Winnicott continually stresses the importance of the natural bond which could and should exist between a mother and baby. He describes it as a 'delicate mechanism' which nothing should be allowed to disturb and which makes possible a relationship that allows the child to flourish through the crucial stages of development.

The maternal instinct is a way of being which ensures the loving, protective and safe nurture of the young. We see this with animals. They make their young their priority, providing first and foremost the warm, accepting presence of the mother's body, together with food and shelter. And, for the most part, in the animal kingdom (where there haven't been disturbing influences), the maternal instinct is alive and well.

AN INSECURE WORLD

However, in the world of human beings, the overriding importance of the maternal instinct is rarely acknowledged and the infant's world is not always the secure environment that it could and should be. There are too many distractions. (Not least books that override our maternal instincts. What hope is there for a baby who isn't allowed to fall asleep in the comfort and safety of its mother's arms?)

Centuries of not being valued for ourselves have prevented us from celebrating our most valuable asset. It is the most beautiful quality and the most important. Where it is alive and well, it provides the infant, the evolving little person (who will one day be an adult), with all they need for healthy balanced growth; all they need to meet an ambivalent world and flourish. However, without this important quality being available, the outcome will be very different.

And it is precisely this quality, a warm accepting presence in the counselling relationship, that influences the outcome and success of the therapy. This 'quality' is the responsibility of the counsellor just as the 'quality' of the parent/child relationship is the responsibility of the parent/adult.

As counsellors we are expected to have addressed, or at least to be aware of and have begun the work of addressing, our own issues during training. In just the same way, parents (and I would include teachers, doctors, nurses and anyone in the helping/ nurturing professions) should be at the very least aware of and addressing their own issues. If not, their issues become their child's (student's, patient's) issues, hence the cycles that get passed from generation to generation in families and society.

Every counselling therapy requires a counsellor to have as their priority the needs of the client; to put our own agenda to one side and respond without judgement but with compassion and kindness. If it's our child, or any child, this is the least we should be doing for them now and for the adult they will one day become.

I know from my own experience of the maternal instinct that it is vitally important for healthy emotional growth. If it is in place and doing its job, everyone is truly blessed – parent and child, because it isn't a one-way street. A happy relationship between parent and child enriches the life of both. Where it doesn't exist, for whatever reason, both lives are diminished and deprived of something immeasurably precious.

The wounding environment which I grew up in, not just of my childhood but adolescence and young adulthood, disempowered me in many ways. Most importantly, it overruled the maternal instinct in me just when my babies and I needed it most. So, to a great extent, both they and I missed out on the relationship that we could and should have enjoyed. As a child, despite the unhappy atmosphere in which I grew up, and despite never experiencing maternal love from my mother, I was aware of experiencing feelings which I would describe as tender and nurturing, towards younger children and animals. In her book, *The Fifth Book of Peace*, Maxine Hong Kingston recalls a time when the spirit of Yin suffused everyone and describes it as a feeling of 'love and peace'. This is exactly how I would describe the feeling and I experienced it as something beautiful in a childhood bereft of beauty. When I was older I recognised it to be what was called the maternal instinct; a beautiful healing energy. No wonder one writer believed it would be the human quality that could save the world.

DELAYED MATERNAL INSTINCT

This feeling was with me when I was expecting my first baby and I knew intuitively not to let anything worry me. This wasn't easy since my natural frame of mind was a negative one. But somehow I knew that, if I worried, my unborn baby would worry too, and I didn't want that to happen. So every time I had a negative thought I quickly replaced it with a positive one.

My first son was born at home and it was a natural but very painful birth. For years afterwards I thought it was the shock of the pain that was responsible for what followed. Two days after having my son, I went downstairs to see my dogs. They had been like children to me and I thought the world of them. When I went to them they were so pleased to see me, but I was surprised and shocked to find that I felt nothing for them. I was bewildered by the lack of feeling in myself and I quickly realised that this lack of feeling, this numbness inside, wasn't just about my dogs, it extended to everything, including my baby and my husband. That lovely feeling I had been aware of in myself from a very young age, which I had expected to be there for my baby, had completely deserted me. I waited for it to come back but it didn't and I realised, when my son was little, what a loss this was for him.

Again it was an intuitive understanding. All I knew was that it made life difficult for him and for me because we weren't *connected* in the way that he needed us to be or the way that I had expected and wanted us to be. He didn't feel secure and wasn't as secure as he needed to be, to successfully and happily negotiate life. It was only as time went on that I realised the enormity of this loss for him. A loss that was to have reverberations for years. But this loss was mine too. Not only did I not feel connected to him, I felt rejected by him. Clarisa Pinkola Estes, in her book *Women Who Run With the Wolves*, talks about this feeling. It is a most wounded place for a woman to be. She cannot give her children what they need, when she herself is in this wounded, wounding place.

Two years later, my daughter was born and there was a partial thawing of the numbness, but only partial. The maternal instinct continued to be overshadowed by the numbness that masked the wound which was responsible for all the accumulated anger and hurt that had been storing up in me throughout my childhood and adolescence. It wasn't until five years later, when my third child was born, that the maternal instinct miraculously returned to do its work. As far as my first two children were concerned, it was a case of better late than never, but the damage was done.

Their foundations were not the secure foundations they could and should have been. I know from my own experience, and the experience of people I have worked with, that it can take the best part of a lifetime to rebuild our own foundations. As with building a house, it is far better to have good foundations in place from the start. But we were lucky that it returned at all. Melanie Klein makes sense to me when she writes that some women intuitively know that there is a beautiful quality locked up in them, which having a baby can release. When it doesn't happen the first time, they go on having another child and then another, in the hope that it will be released. Sadly for some, it never is. But we need to ask ourselves, *how does it get locked away in the first place?*

For years I thought that my numbness and loss of connection to my first two children was due to the shock of the pain of my first labour. Twenty-three years down the line, I remember trying to explain to my eldest son why something had happened to him. I said that I felt that what he had experienced had its roots in how I had been when he was little. I explained that, until now, I had believed that the cause had been the pain of labour, but that recently I had begun to wonder if what had in fact happened was that giving birth had in some inexplicable way made me relive my mother's rejection of me. It was an intuition that was just beginning to filter through, an intuition that was endorsed some weeks later when circumstances allowed me to meaningfully link the gnawing pain I had carried for most of my life with the circumstances of my birth. I was lucky in that I had been aware of the maternal in myself as a child, as an adolescent and while waiting for my first baby to be born. I was lucky too that it hadn't been entirely extinguished. Looking back, I see its naturally occurring presence in me, as a saving grace, in a life that lacked warmth. I knew how I could, should and wanted to feel. The maternal instinct is such an important quality, driven underground or disempowered by early experiences and by a world that does not value it for what it is. And yet it is the guarantor of a healthy mental life for each individual, for society and for life as a whole.

All this happened to me years ago. Life and my intuition gradually revealed the truth of these experiences to me. A truth that was endorsed for me by Deepak Chopra in his book *Ageless Body Timeless Mind* where he suggests that, for a mother with what he calls healthy memories, what I would describe as happy or simply good enough memories of early childhood, the prognosis for a natural and happy bonding with her baby is good, and they will enjoy the flow of mutual love. Sadly though, when the memories are unhappy or not good enough, the precious bonding mechanism may be compromised and these unhappy experiences can trigger depression with symptoms similar to the ones that manifested for me and stayed with me long after the birth of my first baby.

And it isn't only unhappy memories associated with early childhood that can interfere with the delicate bonding mechanism between mother and baby. The problem can be preverbal feelings being triggered and these are very powerful because they happened to us before we had words we could put to them. They are feelings that inhabit the very fabric of our being.

Plato said that experience is knowledge and my experience, my knowledge, showed me how crucially important the maternal instinct is. It wasn't something that was available to me in my childhood and sometimes I do wonder how differently my life and, by extension, the life of my children would have been if I had known the accepting warmth of the maternal in my childhood. I will never know. What I do know though for sure is that losing it, or not having it available to us as infants, can have far-reaching implications for our future well-being.

COUNTERING NEGATIVE BEGINNINGS

What can we do to prevent preverbal feelings and 'outworn memories' seizing a new lease on our lives? One thing we can do is to be aware of how our early experiences continue to exert an influence on us. This makes it important for us to know the circumstances of our birth and be aware of how those circumstances might impact on our lives and our own experience of giving birth and parenting our children. If we are aware of this we can make sense of how we feel especially if we are able to talk to someone and make the necessary connections. Making connections is a powerful way of diffusing the negative energy around our wounds.

Perhaps if I had been able to talk to someone about how I felt after I had my first child, someone with the training to know what to look for, they would have known the importance of exploring past experience and made the all-important connection which would have helped me to understand why I was numb, allowing me to begin the work of healing. In this way, the work of healing destructive childhood experiences can be addressed before they cause more damage.

Recognising the need for a supportive network around the mum-to-be and her baby is crucially important. Giving birth is a life-changing event for everyone involved, with far-reaching effects, especially for the mother and baby. So it becomes vitally important to facilitate the best possible outcome.

Ideally the family network should be our source of support but this isn't always possible or the best option. Where this is the case, what is known as a *doula* could make a difference and make possible a beneficial start for mother and baby. The significant thing about a doula is that she is someone outside the family dynamic who can provide companionship through the pregnancy, labour and the early days of parenthood. She provides physical and emotional support and helps facilitate the best possible outcome for mother and baby. A doula can be hired professionally but there are also agencies including the NHS that have volunteer doulas willing to provide this crucial service.

Strategy for putting a support system in place:

◆ There is a greater awareness now of the phenomenon of post-partum depression and the need to acknowledge this possibility and provide support.
◆ Be aware that there could be some rekindling of early experiences.
◆ Where there were known problems for the mother in her infancy, being ready to make available professional help in the form of counselling would provide a much needed safety net for mother and baby.
◆ Acknowledging and allowing the mother to talk through what she is feeling and explore what's going on for her, will pay dividends in terms of mother and baby's ongoing relationship and emotional well-being.

SELF-COMPASSION

I'd like to add one other thought here which clients and students found helpful even if the concept seemed a little strange initially, and that is that we can be our own best mother. You can access more about this online but where we have missed out on the maternal instinct in our own lives we can practise ways of being that are beneficial to ourselves and our children. Simply put, we can be gentle with ourselves; not beat ourselves up about our perceived shortcomings. Be compassionate and appreciative of ourselves. And above all be kind to ourselves.

Strategy for building self-compassion leading up to and after baby's birth:

- Be gentle with yourself and know that you are doing the most wonderful and amazing thing, in bringing a new life into the world.
- A considerate and supportive network in the months leading up to the birth will benefit you and your baby. If one isn't available, try to give it to yourself as much as you possibly can. You and your baby deserve it.
- Focus on your strengths and blessings – avoid negative thinking at all costs.
- Self-compassion will communicate itself to your baby and so benefit both of you.
- If this becomes a habit before your baby is born it will nurture both of you in the weeks and months after the birth.

In short, anything which allows the maternal instinct to do its vital job is so important and it is important to say, too, that the father can be the provider of this life enhancing energy. In fact it is true to say that in some couples it is the father who carries this tender, nurturing energy. Programmes such as *Long Lost Family* are testament to the fact that non-birth parents can make this nurturing energy available to the children they have adopted. So too can anyone who can afford to be generous with kindness, which is a very similar empowering energy.

So it isn't exclusive to mothers but, where a mother is free to make it available to her child, it is the most precious gift she can give them and it will be their companion and strength throughout their life.

THE MATERNAL INSTINCT – SUMMARIES

◆ Probably the most important quality we will ever experience in ourselves or another.

◆ Described as a delicate mechanism, nothing should be allowed to disturb it.

◆ The maternal instinct is the guarantor of the safe, loving nurture of the young.

◆ A happy relationship between parent and child enriches the life of both.

◆ The maternal instinct can be disempowered by the early experiences of the mother and by a world that doesn't value it for what it is.

◆ The absence of this relationship can have far-reaching implications for a child.

◆ We should be aware how early experiences can continue to exert an influence on us.

◆ Giving birth is a life-changing experience. The new mother needs a support network for herself and her baby.

◆ Where needed, a doula can make all the difference for mother and baby.

◆ We can be our own best mother.

◆ Fathers can also provide this nurturing energy as can adoptive parents.

◆ The mother's energy of love and peace is a most precious gift.

6

THE FAMILY

'Take care of the family and the rest will care for itself.'
Clifford Longley

'It has been found that those children who grow up in homes where there is love and affection, have a healthier physical development and study better at school. Conversely, those who lack human affection have more difficulty in developing physically and mentally. These children also find it difficult to show affection when they grow up, which is such a great tragedy.'
Dalai Lama

The family that we grow up in, whether it is a traditional family or not, will have an enduring influence on the way in which we negotiate the world. It can literally make or break us. How we are received by our first family, loved or rejected, respected or abused – these scenarios constitute the blueprint of our future. What we experience as someone's child, brother, sister, nephew, niece or grandchild, is carried with us into the outside world. It colours our experience in the world and has inescapable implications for what we find there, not least because at some level every situation we go into replays the family dynamic, so that where we are in our family will influence what we find in these other situations.

If we were respected and valued in our family we will expect to be respected and valued in society but if we weren't then it's unlikely that we will expect to be respected and valued in the outside world. If we weren't listened to in our family the chances are that we won't expect to be listened to at school or in the workplace. Likewise, if sadly we are the scapegoat in our family, we may find ourselves being the scapegoat in other areas of our life. To a certain extent we draw these experiences to ourselves so that they become a self-fulfilling prophecy, one that was not of our initial making. As children we cannot be expected to understand what's happening to us, but later, as we become more aware of how we feel in our day to day life, it is very important to consider where we were in our family setting and how it influences the present. Only then can we decide whether we are happy with the influence it has on us, or whether that influence is detrimental and something we need to change.

If we decide that we want to change, then it would be a good idea to sit down with some appropriate self-help books or look for a counsellor. In counselling clients are respected and valued and above all listened to. This alone can make counselling a powerful healing experience. Or you can do what Adler suggested and when you go out into the world act 'as if' you expect to be respected and listened to. Respect and attentive listening are cornerstones of Person Centred Therapy. Respect for the person you are talking to coupled with acceptance of that person, whoever they are, contributes to their experience of being valued and actually listened to, as if they mattered – which is of itself a healing and empowering experience. We are always being told not to take ourselves too seriously but this is perhaps one time when we should, so that this too can become a self-fulfilling prophecy in our lives. It isn't only negative states that can become self-fulfilling prophecies.

However, there is very little if anything that children can do about an unhappy or abusive family life and if you are going out into the world from such a situation, you feel worthless and unacceptable. And as if that wasn't enough, the simplest slight or rejection, something as simple as a smile not returned, reinforces the fundamental worthlessness that has been written into your foundations.

HARMFUL CHILDHOODS

So to say that family life is important is an understatement. It can literally make the difference between life and death. There are many unsuccessful attempts at suicide. Each one is a cry for help and it never ceases to amaze me how many people reach out to the world in this way and not be asked why? I have worked with several people who, in their past, had made suicide attempts which resulted in them being taken to hospital. Not one of them was asked why they did it. Not by the hospital or their families. It seems that people would rather not have that question answered. Or perhaps, in the case of the families, they know the answer but they just don't want to face the facts. Which is why, in counselling, it is not only appropriate but also extremely important to ask why, and to listen, so that at last experiences can be heard and acknowledged for what they are and for the way in which they have affected a life.

When I took an overdose of aspirin and told my parents, nothing was done. I put myself to bed and drifted in and out of consciousness for three days and in the moments of consciousness I couldn't escape the deafening sound of clanging bells in my head. On the fourth day I got up and went to work, to a new job that I'd started the previous Monday. My cry for help, because I'm sure that's what it was, had taken place on Thursday evening, so I had missed the Friday of my first week. I shall never forget my immediate boss saying to me that I mustn't feel bad about missing a day of my first week, I wasn't to worry about it, it didn't matter. I remember looking at her and thinking that I hadn't given it a thought but how kind she was to want to reassure me.

As I've mentioned before, a child that isn't wanted has that rejection imprinted in their psyche. Where this is the case there can be a tape playing in the background of their mind telling them that they aren't wanted and shouldn't be here, which is constantly reinforced by the thoughtlessness of others.

That isn't to say that this message cannot eventually be wiped off the psyche; it can, as it was for me, by the simple but profound act of writing a letter. But it would save a great deal of anguish for everyone if the message wasn't there in the first place. To be an unwanted child is to arrive in the world with an enormous disadvantage. That isn't to say that everyone who has an unhappy childhood is going to attempt or commit suicide. But suicide comes in many guises and it can be a long and drawn-out affair: anorexia, bulimia, self-harm, addiction, the list goes on, and it doesn't have to. In his book, *The Making and Breaking of Affectional Bonds*, John Bowlby writes that depressive illnesses in adult life can be the result of unhappy experiences in early childhood.

He adds that very often children don't have the opportunity to express feelings or ask questions of a sympathetic adult, so that these feelings and unanswered questions, together with their harmful effects, are stored in every cell of the immature infant and child, and exert a crippling influence. These affects may eventually find resolution in understanding, or love, or fulfilment in some area of life. But even such resolution, indispensable as it is for the remainder of a person's life, cannot give back, or make up for, what was lost in those intervening years.

THE ROAD TO HEALING

The fact is that most people would prefer to forget what it was to be a child in an unhappy family home. To remember and acknowledge such a childhood isn't easy. But we can't forget it; it is always there. So to acknowledge it and find resolution in some way is crucially important for the remainder of our life.

However, there are stumbling blocks to this healing endeavour. It isn't easy to admit, even to yourself, that your parents could be unkind to you. As Bowlby says, parents themselves aren't likely to encourage this exploration of events and feelings. It is also painful for parents to admit to themselves, let alone anyone else, that they were less than loving to their children. Added to these constraints is very often a family myth which bears little resemblance to the facts. I remember hearing my sister say to my mother that she would always remember what a happy childhood she'd had. I couldn't believe what I was hearing and, without thinking, for once spoke my truth. I said that I hadn't had a happy childhood and wouldn't forget how unhappy it had been. My mother and sister looked at me and burst into tears but all I had done was speak the truth. I hadn't kept to the family myth that we were a happy family. Again, this isn't about blame. Blame doesn't get us anywhere. It's about being honest. With honesty we can get to a place where we can improve how young lives fulfil themselves.

LESLIE'S STORY

In his book, *Emotional Intelligence*, Daniel Goleman endorses the crucial influence that our first family has on us, for better or worse. He calls the following extract, a 'low key family tragedy', a *'frequently'* repeated childhood experience.

'Carl and Ann are showing their daughter Leslie, just five, how to play a brand new video game. But as Leslie starts to play, her parents' overly eager attempts to "help" her just seem to get in the way. Contradictory orders fly in every direction.

"To the right, to the right – stop. Stop. Stop!" Ann, the mother, urges, her voice growing more intent and anxious as Leslie, sucking on her lip and staring wide-eyed at the video screen, struggles to follow these directives.

"See, you're not lined up... put it to the left! To the left!" Carl, the girl's Father brusquely orders.

Meanwhile Ann, her eyes rolling upward in frustration, yells over his advice, "Stop! Stop!"

Leslie, unable to please either her father or her mother, contorts her jaw in tension and blinks as her eyes fill with tears.

Her parents start bickering, ignoring Leslie's tears. "She's not moving the stick *that* much!" Ann tells Carl, exasperated.

As the tears start rolling down Leslie's cheeks, neither parent makes any move that indicates they notice or care. As Leslie raises her hand to wipe her eyes, her father snaps, "Okay, put your hand back on the stick... you wanna get ready to shoot. Okay, put it over!" And her mother barks, "Okay, move it just a teeny bit!"

But by now Leslie is sobbing softly, alone with her anguish.' [3]

Leslie feels so alone. So forgotten. And she is alone and forgotten with two people who are intent on their own conflict with each other, who only refer back to her by way of gaining ammunition for themselves. Goleman says that at such times children 'learn deep lessons.' The lesson that is learned, especially when this scenario is repeated as it is for many children, is that no one cares about their feelings and by extension themselves. Not a happy or helpful message to carry with you into the outside world.

FUTURE SUCCESS

Importantly, carrying such a message from our parents into the world has implications for success in school and throughout life. Even more importantly, it will have an effect on the way we treat our own children unless we wake up to what we are doing. My first son was about six when I realised one day that my husband and I were, at times, treating him in the same critical way that my parents had treated my brother. It was an uncomfortable moment when I realised the similarity between my parents' attitude and ours, and it was a crucially important moment of self-awareness. It is vitally important that we wake up to what we are doing to our children because '...if we become conscious of what we are doing, we then have the chance to free ourselves from the constrictions of our past.' [4] and where necessary, we can change our tapes from the ones we were programmed with.

To a very great extent, whether we can hope to succeed or fail in life is rooted in the early years of our lives and, surprising as it may seem, success isn't dependent on IQ so much as emotional security and stability. This security and stability comes naturally from being nurtured within a relationship and atmosphere of mutual love and respect. It is this secure emotional centre that fosters the ability to learn. Goleman adds that every child needs to receive the necessary help to have within themselves a healthy 'emotional repertoire'. But if we are to teach such a repertoire to our children we must first be taught it, or learn it for ourselves, as soon as we possibly can.

Strategy: There are steps we can take to help ourselves change our programming and these can be done on our own or to augment the longer term work we might be doing with a counsellor:

- Become aware of your self-talk, it probably isn't helpful and so needs to change.
- Use different words. Words are so powerful, especially when directed at the self or the evolving and vulnerable child.
- Watch your emotions and your responses to your emotions.
- Stop negative thoughts in their tracks and replace them with a positive thought.
- Silence the internal critical voice. It's an intruder that you definitely do not need or deserve.
- Cultivate cheerfulness. Smile on the outside and the inside will soon follow.
- Count your blessings while remembering that the little things aren't little; they are very important.
- Look up self-help strategies online and experiment with them. You may find you enjoy these exercises and will be surprised by the results.

◆ There is a lot at stake here, for you and the child in your care.

PTSD AND CHILDHOOD TRAUMAS

The need for us to cultivate a healthy emotional repertoire is emphasised by work done on post-traumatic stress disorder. People suffering from PTSD have one thing in common: they had no control over the trauma. This 'not being in control of what happens' has a biological impact on the workings of the brain. This is equally true for children who are quite literally 'trapped' in their family setting. They have no influence on it and no control over what happens to them. Trapped as many children are in a less than happy family situation, they feel an almost permanent sense of anxiety and the need to be on the alert. Such a situation compromises concentration and learning, and every other aspect of a child's life.

Compromised concentration and learning can be carried from childhood into adult life. Where this is the case Cognitive Behavioural Therapy could be of help. It is a therapy which looks at both thought and behaviour patterns and provides coping skills to mitigate the effects of PTSD in daily life. Psychodynamic or Person Centred counselling can also play an important role since the telling and understanding of a person's story can lessen the impact of the anxiety and flashbacks which are symptomatic of the condition. PTSD occurs because things happen over which the victim had no control; they were vulnerable and powerless to defend themselves. Understanding this and initiating healing and change for themselves is a powerful first step in taking back control.

In finding a link between people with PTSD and childhood experience, Daniel Goleman says, 'The more ordinary travails of childhood, such as being chronically ignored and deprived of attention or tenderness by one's parents, abandonment or loss, or social rejection may never reach the fever pitch of trauma, but they surely leave their imprint on the emotional brain, creating distortions – and tears and rages – in intimate relationships later in life.' (5)

These tears and rages in intimate relationships later in life are something that many people experience. Maybe it wasn't safe to express anger and hurt in their family setting so that it is only in an adult relationship of perceived trust that they can be expressed or at least no longer be held in check. It can come as much a surprise to the one expressing the anger as it is to the one who has to live with it. What is hurting here is the child in you, your inner child, the hurt child who needs your attention. We must attend to this child if we are to put a stop to the wounded self, wounding others.

There are resonances here of the inner child, who always comes into the counselling session needing to be acknowledged and heard.

THE FAMILY – SUMMARIES

◆ A kind and nurturing family life is the best guarantor of a healthy mental outlook in adult life.
◆ How we are treated by our family can colour our experiences in the outside world.
◆ We need to consider how our place in the family influences our present life.

◆ What we are aware of, we can change. It isn't only negative states that can become self-fulfilling prophecies.

◆ Attempted suicide is a cry for help. Experiences need to be heard and acknowledged.

◆ Feelings that can't be expressed can be stored in the body and exert a crippling influence.

◆ Finding resolution/healing for an unhappy childhood is crucially important for the rest of a person's life.

◆ The myth of a happy family is powerful even in unhappy family lives.

◆ Success may be more dependent on emotional security and stability than IQ.

◆ Children trapped in an unhappy family environment can suffer the crippling effects of PTSD.

7

BORN BEAUTIFUL

'Whatever we put into a child's soul we naturally will find there...'

Alice Miller

In a radio interview, one of Coco the Clown's daughters said that her father believed there were no bad children, only bad parents. Nicolai Poliakoff loved children and his commitment to children's charities – and in particular in promoting road safety for children, for which he was awarded the OBE – bore witness to that commitment.

So would you agree with him or would it be fairer to say, 'There are no bad children, only bad parenting'? If this is closer to the truth, why is it? Is it because, for the most important job we will ever do, we have no training at all? Would it be true to say that, for the most part, we mother and father as we were mothered and fathered? If this is true, then many of us are doing the most important job of our life with an enormous handicap.

Child and family psychiatrist John Bowlby endorsed what many of us have experienced for ourselves, saying that we expect and want to be good parents and then we find (if we are honest with ourselves) that we aren't doing a very good job. He explains that our ability to parent can be 'distorted' by our own experiences in infancy and childhood. The tragedy is that we don't even realise it before the damage is done, as the mistakes of previous generations are inevitably passed on.

There is nothing new about this. It has been the way of things, generation after generation. I remember reading that what we ignore in ourselves 'returns to haunt us through our children'. [2] Our present society is expressing this truth loud and clear and we can't keep ignoring the evidence, which is all around us.

EMOTIONAL HEALTH

Try as we might, we cannot escape the fact that we are as responsible for our child's emotional health as we are for their physical well-being. Parents and carers are the guardians of the emotional and mental health of the infant, child, adolescent and adult, and, by extension, of society itself. It is an enormous responsibility that cultures, societies and individuals appear to overlook. It is a crucial issue and yet you won't find any mention of this in the literature that new parents receive. I have looked in vain for the words that say 'Your child's physical well-being is important but equally important is your child's emotional and mental well-being. The outcome of the rest of her life depends on how you treat her in infancy and childhood. You must know what you are doing. If you don't know, then perhaps you can be forgiven for what you do. But once you know, and you should want to know, there's no longer a choice.'

Importantly, our child's emotional health will depend to a great extent on our own emotional health. So it is crucial for us to become aware of what motivates and influences us. Once we are aware, we can choose our responses and act out of love rather than anger, or any of the other conditioned responses, which we use automatically and which can be so damaging for children and our relationship with them.

We don't have to go on, generation after generation, consciously or unconsciously passing on incapacitating patterns of behaviour. We can change but change means that we have to look honestly at what is happening and then we have to *want* to do things differently.

And while it is possible to achieve this on our own, given the time and the commitment, we can achieve a better and quicker outcome by sitting down with a counsellor who will encourage us to tell our story, the story only we can tell, about how life was for us, so that we can look honestly at how we are, why we are the way we are and where we need to make changes for ourselves and for those whose lives we touch.

The messages that we receive at a preverbal level – that is, in infancy, before we can speak ourselves – are extraordinarily powerful. How we are in the world and how we feel about ourselves comes to us initially and powerfully from the arms that hold us, the words which are spoken to us and the atmosphere in which we develop. And these messages follow us throughout our lives, exerting their influence, for better or worse.

Strategy: How to notice our deep emotional response to certain stimuli:

- We need to become aware of how we engage with our world.
- We need to notice and not be in denial about our deep emotional responses and be prepared to accept that our

emotional response to certain circumstances or triggers may be out of proportion to what has actually occurred in the here and now.

◆ We have to be aware and care about the affect they have on us, how they make us feel, and the affect they have on ourselves and others, how they make us act and the impact of those actions on other precious lives.

◆ Some will almost certainly be detrimental to ourselves and the lives of those around us.

◆ Then we have to want to do things differently. We don't want to feel this pain in ourselves and we don't want to hurt others because of the pain we carry at a deep level.

◆ Knowing our 'story' can help us link certain feelings to early childhood experiences and begin the work of healing and change. However, if we don't know our story, the emotions and the feelings evoked must still be acknowledged and worked through, so that they stop getting in our way and hurting those whose lives we touch.

VICIOUS CIRCLE

I remember walking into university one morning with another mature student at the beginning of the second year and saying to him that, despite trying to treat my children differently from the way my parents had treated me, somehow history had repeated itself by another route. I said it was like a vicious circle, one that I hadn't managed to avoid. Amongst other things, I'd had my own idea of what a perfect childhood should be (everything that mine hadn't been). But while my children were trying to fit in with my idea of their perfect childhood, they couldn't be themselves.

Then in my first term of counsellor training I was introduced to Alice Millar's book *The Drama of Being a Child*, a book which should be read by anyone involved with children in any way. To my surprise, I found a chapter entitled 'The Vicious Circle of Contempt' and what she had to say was compelling. Even so, I wouldn't describe this circle as one of contempt. It is a vicious circle but, for most of us, it is a circle of unawareness.

We need to become aware of how completely our early life influences the present moment: how it affects us at a deep unconscious level and has a profound effect on relationships of every kind.

I became aware of this one day as two of my children, then aged four and two, were innocently playing. I don't remember why but I was shouting at them, raging just as our mother used to do to us. We would be playing, when suddenly she would be there shouting at us, red-faced with anger which we couldn't possibly have been the cause of. I can still remember how the little child in me felt. The bewilderment at what was happening, coupled with my child's inner knowing that we hadn't really done anything wrong. Even so, there was no escape from her torrent of anger, from her wounded and wounding rage.

That moment when I was shouting at my children was a crucial one. Something in me said, 'Jane, where can you go from here?' It was a turning point. I realised I was doing to them what had been done to me. They weren't the cause of my anger but they were the defenceless recipients of it, just as we had been with our mother. This was exactly the opposite of what I wanted. I didn't want them to live on the receiving end of my hurt and anger, as we had lived on the receiving end of our mother's.

In those days though, there wasn't the help available that there is today. So for me it took another thirteen years, consciously working alone, followed by five years of grieving, to exorcise the anger that was stored in me. And this taught me something important about grief. While we work through the pain of the overt loss, at other levels in our psyche earlier traumas are also being worked through. So in some paradoxical way, we can come out of grief, healed at other levels of our being.

Strategy: It isn't easy to turn anger into compassion in the moment that we are engulfed in it but turn it we must, if we don't want to cause years of damage.

- Wanting to, is the first step.
- So, ahead of possible upsets to which we might overreact, we should concentrate on the *intention* not to be ruled by our anger. We resolve to control it, and refuse to allow it to control us.
- Our motivation for taking this step must be that we don't want to hurt anyone, especially the children in our care.
- It will require a sustained effort but it's worth it.
- Exploring mindfulness and what it can contribute to our endeavour will provide us with effective tools.

However, the important thing is for the damage not to be done in the first place. There are, of course, life events that we cannot avoid but there is so much that could be avoided, and there is so much to be gained, as individuals, as family and as a society. 'What a wonderful world it will be when children are born into loving nurturing environments. Then adulthood can be spent evolving, rather than trying to release painful conditioning from the past.' (3)

BORN BEAUTIFUL – SUMMARIES

◆ For the most important job we will ever do we have no training at all.

◆ Our ability to parent can be distorted by our experiences in infancy and childhood.

◆ We are the guardians of our child's emotional and mental health.

◆ Our own emotional and mental health will impact our parenting.

◆ The messages we receive at a preverbal level are extraordinarily powerful.

◆ There is so much at stake in our relationship with our child.

◆ We can repeat patterns from our childhood without realising it.

◆ We need to be aware how completely our early life influences the present.

8

OEDIPUS AND FREUD
REVISITED

'One has to ask oneself… how much of the Oedipus complex is really inherited. And how much is passed on by tradition from one generation to the other.'

Ferenczi

'Demanding more from you than I'm willing to give to you breeds resentment.'

Daniels and Horowitz

In chapter 3, 'The Simple Needs of the Baby', I introduced you to the positive view of infant development given to us by Suttie, Bowlby and Brazelton. In the place of original sin, that pervasive notion instilled into the human psyche by the Church, Ian Suttie affirms that the primordial impulse is love. This is what his work with mothers and babies showed him, what he believed a baby brings with her into life. Similarly, John Bowlby believed that we came into life with an innate morality when he wrote, 'It is a notion which puts beside the concept of original sin, of which psychoanalysis discovers much evidence in the human heart, the concept of original concern for others or original goodness which, if given favourable circumstances, will gain the upper hand. It is a cautiously optimistic view of human nature, and one that I believe to be justified.' (3)

Those words 'given favourable circumstances' are so important. So is the positive approach to child development that these three men share. And it is important to keep this positive approach in mind because so much is projected onto children, both by religion in the notion of original sin and by psychiatry, as mentioned by Bowlby, both of which I think have contributed to a debilitating legacy. It is this legacy that I want to look at in this chapter, to consider how unhelpful it has been to attitudes of infant development (infants who will one day be teenagers, adults and parents, for whom those attitudes can have had long-term debilitating affects), beginning with the Oedipus myth and the interpretation that Freud attributed to it.

THE STORY OF OEDIPUS

According to the myth, Oedipus was born the son of King Laius and Queen Jocasta. While Oedipus was still a baby, Laius was told that his son would grow up and kill him. With Jocasta's co-operation, Oedipus's ankles were broken and he was abandoned on Mount Cithaeron to be eaten by birds of prey. However, he was found by a kindly shepherd and taken back to Corinth where he was raised as the child of King Polybus and his Queen.

When a young man, Oedipus was told that he would murder his father. Believing that King Polybus was his father, and being a loving son, he left Corinth so that the prophecy couldn't be fulfilled. As he journeyed he was accosted by another traveller; they fought and Oedipus killed his opponent. He travelled on and reached Thebes, a city beset by a plague from which it could only be freed by the solving of a riddle. Oedipus solved this riddle and in doing so won the hand of the recently widowed queen, who subsequently bore him children.

Eventually, Oedipus found out that the stranger on the road who had accosted him, who he had killed, was his true father and that the woman he had married was his mother. He was beside himself with grief and shame. In an attempt to overcome these unbearable feelings he blinded himself and spent the remainder of his life as a poor beggar.

OEDIPUS INTERPRETED

I don't know what you make of the Oedipus myth, bearing in mind that it is just a myth, but I want to focus on the integrity of Oedipus, the integrity of the child. His parents, in their fear, were prepared to leave him to a cruel fate. As a young man, he left King Polybus and his Queen, the only parents he'd known, to avoid hurting them by fulfilling the prophecy he'd been given. In those days travelling was a dangerous undertaking; if someone accosted you, you defended yourself and asked questions later.

In short, he didn't set out to kill Laius; it was Laius himself who invited the confrontation. Nor did he set out to marry his mother. The queen's hand in marriage was the reward already decreed to whoever solved the riddle of the Sphinx. When he found out that he had married his mother he punished himself severely. How then, did Freud manage to make Oedipus into a baddy? Why protect the parents at the expense of the defenceless infant? Freud must have known from his own experience and from the experience of his patients that the prime cause of psychic distress and emotional illness stems from treatment received in infancy and early childhood.

Given the 'facts' of the myth, how did Freud manage to come up with a theory suggesting that children harbour sexual desires towards their parents and that failure to satisfy these desires leads to unresolved conflicts and neurotic symptoms; personality dysfunctions that could impede the rest of a person's life?

FICTITIOUS LABELS AND REAL PAIN

Even more troubling than these theories are in themselves, is the fact that such terms as *Oedipal conflict*, *Oedipal rivalry* and *Oedipal complex* have been imposed on unsuspecting and trusting clients who deserve better. By using these fictitious labels, because that's what they are, therapists and counsellors have somehow put the blame on the child and in doing so they under-rate the very real pain that clients carry and its true origin. In doing so, the original wounding is not being identified and acknowledged, and while it isn't acknowledged, the healing process is impeded.

What I hear in the Oedipus myth is that children will take the blame for their parents' failures on themselves. Clients usually have great difficulty in apportioning blame to a parent or parents and in coming to look honestly at the implications of the treatment they received. As always, this isn't about blame; it's about freeing the self from unjust blame and guilt, so as to live more freely and meaningfully in their own lives.

What I know from my own experience, from my children's experience and from friends, acquaintances and clients, is that children are endlessly forgiving. They move on from harsh or thoughtless treatment, able somehow to meet life fresh in each moment, only in some cases to be crushed again.

The following quote from Marie Cardinal encapsulates much of what I've been saying. As a child she remembers watching her mother 'consoling herself' with wine. She writes: 'I wanted to be the wine, to do her some good… to make her happy, to attract her attention. I promised myself I would find her a treasure… What a surprise she would have! Her face would relax, she would kiss me, she would love me.' (4)

How sad for Marie's mother, that she didn't realise that her treasure was Marie herself. Sad too for Marie, as her efforts were rejected by her wounded and wounding mother. Cardinal concludes: 'My love was not, apparently, the right key… All these fruitless efforts had made me reject myself; I was ashamed.' (5)

LITTLE HANS AND DORA

In the light of all this I want to look at the way in which Freud responded to two children who he was asked to analyse. Both were believed to have problems that Freud would be able to resolve. The problems are very definitely with the adults in their lives but, as you will see, Freud used them to 'prove' his theory while ignoring the very real distress that was being caused in their young lives by the very people they should have been able to trust.

Sad to say that often, as parents, we expect more from our children than we do from ourselves. We often expect more from our children than we actually give to them. The reason for introducing Little Hans and Dora to you is that their stories illustrate so clearly the plight of the child in an adult world. One aspect of this is the way in which some adults are prepared to use children, often without realising what they are doing, as a means to their own ends.

THE GOOSE GIRL

But first I want to tell you a fairy story because it illustrates another very important point, which is that every child needs at least one *good* adult in their lives, whether that is a parent, teacher, aunt, uncle, neighbour or friend. Remember the little heroes and heroines of Dickens's novels. He must have been acutely aware of the plight of the child in an adult world; so many of his novels revolve around children thoughtlessly or cruelly treated by the adults in their lives. Without that minimum one good adult, a child is truly lost in a hostile world.

The story of *The Goose Girl* tells of an old queen who has to send her only daughter on a long journey to meet and marry her future husband. Amongst the items the young princess is given are a talking horse and a handkerchief with three drops of the queen's blood on it, and she has a maid with her for company. In the course of the journey she loses the handkerchief, which represents the loss of her inner resources. (This can happen to us on our journey through infancy and childhood.) This dis-empowered her (as it disempowers us so that other people can have an overwhelming influence on us) to such an extent that the scheming maid was able to force her to swap places and make her swear not to tell anyone what had happened when they arrived at the royal court. As a result of this, the princess was taken for a maid and given the task of helping to look after the geese. The maid who had taken her place was treated like a princess and when she asked for the talking horse's head to be cut off (to prevent it giving her away), her request was granted and all hope for the princess lost.

The King realised that all was not well with the little goose girl and asked her what was troubling her. She couldn't tell him because she had promised not to. The King suggested that there was no harm in her telling her troubles to the hearth. Hiding behind the hearth the King was able to hear her story and learn the truth of what had happened and being a *good* King, he reinstated her to her rightful place as his son's future bride.

THE GOOSE GIRL INTERPRETED

Something else comes to mind as I write this, which is that, for the most part, children don't tell anyone how they are being treated by certain people in their lives. They probably couldn't put it into words even if they wanted to. Just as the princess was disempowered by the maid and sworn to secrecy, so too there is an unstated but powerful understanding between adult and child, which allows the parent or another adult complete licence, while the child remains endlessly forgiving and loyal, at great cost to themselves.

For me, the way in which the princess was sent into the world, without the inner resources to cope, is crucially important. It represents the way in which the majority of children are sent into the world and expected to cope with far more than it is reasonable or kind to expect of them. If we are unlucky, our parents' criticism and harshness disempowers us and follows us out into the world and, before we realise it, we will have passed these debilitating pressures onto our children. The princess was trapped in circumstances beyond her control, as children can be, and the one good adult in her life was her salvation. This emphasises the way in which the good adults in our lives are so important: they are kind, see us as ourselves, care enough to notice when all is not well, and take the trouble to find out what is hurting.

LITTLE HANS

The case of Little Hans shows clearly how a child is a victim of his parents' upbringing and ambitions. Not that his parents were bad people, but they were both out of touch with the world of their child, incapable of an empathic relationship with him, and obviously cut off from the child in themselves. In addition to this, sadly, their own agendas prevented them from seeing and responding to the needs of their little boy. But let me give you a precis of the case study and you can draw your own conclusions.

Little Hans's 'trouble' was triggered by an incident which took place when he was out with his mother. A tram horse stumbled and fell in front of him. Today, this would be equivalent to a five-year-old child out shopping with its mother, and having a road traffic accident happen right next to where he was standing. A traumatic experience to say the least. Frightening and disturbing for the adults around, let alone a little five-year-old. Imagine the enormous horse and the screams of the people. And yet, when his mother got in, she was so unaware of the impact this incident might have had on her little boy that she didn't even mention to anyone what had happened. The trauma that Hans had experienced wasn't acknowledged and he was left to cope with it alone.

The way he dealt with this trauma was to refuse to go out of the house. Some of us wouldn't be surprised by this at all, but for his father, who was an admirer of Freud, it was an opportunity to ingratiate himself with Freud, and an opportunity for Freud to fit the little boy into his theories. The injustice that was done to Hans has been perpetuated by generations of Freudian students with theories of infantile sexuality and Oedipal issues, all Freudian constructs, distracting attention from what really happened.

Instead of acknowledging that Hans had witnessed a frightening incident which could result in him not wanting to go out into the streets (for fear of it happening again), Freud's theory maintained that Hans's mother had become the object of his libido so that he didn't want to leave her, which fitted neatly with his views on infant sexuality. Also it was 'obvious' to them all that he wanted his father out of the way. That fits conveniently with Freud's Oedipal theory. But what an enormous injustice was done to Hans. And continues to be done by adults with their own agenda who are out of touch with what it is to be a child. Even today, this idea that the child is some way at fault, with no attempt to acknowledge or understand the impact of certain experiences, permeates a great deal of psychoanalytic thinking, thinking that then passes into the social psyche.

DORA

Just like Little Hans, Dora was trapped in a world of adults who were happy to exploit her for their own ends. Freud described this case study as the 'treatment of a hysterical girl'. When you have read what follows, you may wish to describe her not as a hysterical girl but as a vulnerable and exploited child. Although there are times when he seems to forget it himself, Freud does in fact stress that, more than anything else, the family circumstances should be taken into consideration with the problems that children have. So often it is family circumstances which are the cause of stress, illness and anti-social behaviour in children of all ages.

So what were the 'family circumstances' that Dora found herself in? Let us look at each of the adults in her life in turn so that we have an idea of what she was up against. Freud tells us that her mother was 'uncultivated' and 'foolish'. He uses the words 'house-wife psychosis' to describe her preoccupation with the affairs of the home. She was obsessional about cleanliness and made it impossible for the house and its contents to be enjoyed. Such a preoccupation wouldn't leave much time for her children, so it isn't surprising that Freud tells us that Dora's relationship with her mother was strained and unfriendly. Under any circumstances, having a mother so preoccupied would have been a great loss to Dora as a child and adolescent but it also left her totally exposed to exploitation by her father and other important and powerful adults in her life.

Her relationship with her father was not a simple one. Distanced from his wife (partly because he had contracted syphilis before they were married and subsequently infected her), he allowed Dora to nurse him through his frequent illnesses and used her has a confidante. Both roles would have been a heavy burden for a young girl, however willingly undertaken for a loved father. There was no doubt that Dora loved her father very much; perhaps he was all the more important because her mother was emotionally absent. So it will have come as a bitter blow to her when her place was taken in the sick room by Frau K., a woman who was bored with her own husband and flattered by Dora's father's maturity, gifts and attention.

Frau K. originally befriended Dora when the two families first met. Dora, who had received very little mothering herself, was like a 'mother' to Frau K's two young children. Like Dora's father, Frau K. made Dora her confidante, sharing with Dora her dissatisfaction with her marriage. However, once she had gained access to the affections of Dora's father, she had little use for her former confidante – unlike her husband Herr K., who saw the potential in Dora when she was only fourteen.

A twenty-seven-year-old man must have appeared quite old to the fourteen-year-old Dora. Not surprisingly, when his attentions to her became sexual, she resisted and appealed to her parents for protection. However, her father was happy to accept Herr K.'s denial that he had made advances to her, since he didn't want his relationship with Frau K. to be disturbed. He made the excuse that Frau K. was unhappy with her husband and that he didn't want to cause her any additional pain, and yet he had been blind to his daughter's pain for years. He asked Freud to 'reason' with Dora, and yet he himself was not prepared to listen to her, let alone protect her.

After Herr K.'s initial advances, Dora was careful not to be left alone with him. A precaution that we might think was entirely sensible, but Freud described her behaviour as 'completely hysterical' adding that a 'healthy girl' would have found the experience enjoyable. Freud talked about the *temptation* of Herr K.'s presence to Dora, when clearly she felt his presence as a *threat*.

The unfortunate Dora couldn't look anywhere for goodness from the adult world around her. Unlike the goose girl in our fairy story, she doesn't appear to have had that necessary one good adult in her life. Even her last governess used her relationship with Dora as a means of engaging her father's attention and had no real affection for the girl herself. It seems to me that Dora was kind-hearted, insightful and sensible, endlessly seeking and hoping to find friendship and warmth. Yet at every turn she was exploited. However, it is to Dora's enduring credit that she eventually had the strength of character to extricate herself from Freud's accusations and conjectures, and from the analysis that her father had hoped would help her 'to see reason'!

SETTING ASIDE AGENDAS

In so many ways the experiences of Little Hans and Dora bring home to us the void which can exist between the world of the child and the world of the adult. This is extraordinary since each of us was once a child. So we need to make a conscious effort to find out what's happening to our children. To ask them how life is for them and to listen to what they have to say.

And learning to listen is fundamental to our counselling training. You wouldn't think that we needed to be trained to simply listen but it is a very necessary part of the training. Interestingly, something you learn along with that is that most people (including ourselves initially) don't listen attentively to what is being said to them. Our heads are too full of what concerns us. To listen properly, we have to put our own agenda aside. We have to focus our undivided attention on the person talking to us, without constantly turning the conversation back to ourselves. The well-being of the person we are listening to is our prime concern and it makes our engagement with them so much more satisfying and meaningful for us and for them. It can be the start of their healing journey. Don't ever underestimate the power of really listening to another person, especially your child or the child who needs you to listen to them.

Strategy: Steps to take to really listen to your child:

◆ As always the first step is to want to. To want to give your child the precious gift of your time and undivided attention.

◆ Empathy and compassion are two indispensable qualities in a counsellor and are even more important in a parent. If they are available to your child now, the counsellor won't be needed later on.

◆ Really 'see' your child by putting your own agenda/needs aside for the moment.

◆ Ask gentle questions and give time for them to be answered.

◆ Allow feelings to be expressed, acknowledged and believed.

◆ Don't overreact to anything your child says. You want them to feel safe and to feel they can trust you.

◆ Don't self-refer; that is, don't turn the conversation back to you and how things are/were for you, as happens so much in everyday conversation. If you do this it means that you aren't really listening to how life is for your child; instead you are focusing on yourself. There will be time later for you to share your own experiences if you think it will be of help to them.

◆ Most importantly, your commitment to the immediate and long-term well-being of your child or the child in your care must be your primary motivation.

OEDIPUS AND FREUD REVISITED – SUMMARIES

◆ The primordial impulse is love.
◆ Original goodness replaces original sin.

- Have the Church and psychoanalysis left us with a debilitating legacy?
- An alternative view of the Oedipus myth.
- Fictitious labels do clients a disservice.
- Children are endlessly forgiving.
- We can (wrongly) expect more from children than we do from ourselves.
- Children can (wrongly) just be a means to an end.
- Every child needs a minimum one good adult in their life.
- Often children are sent out into the world without the inner resources to cope.
- We need to acknowledge the effect of any trauma.
- We need to make a conscious effort to find out what's happening to our children.
- Ask them how life is for them and really listen to what they have to say, putting our own agenda aside.
- Don't ever underestimate the power of really listening to another person, especially the child who needs you to listen to them.

9

THE IMPORTANCE
OF KINDNESS

*'Kindness is a language all men understand. It breaks down
barriers; it helps people to hope again; it restores their faith
in their fellows.'*

W. E. Sangster

'To re-awaken at kindness…'

Philip Larkin

*'… we may have a fundamental obligation to be kind and
considerate in dealing with children – to care for them – and
to put ourselves out in ways that differ from those in which
we must put ourselves out for adults.'*

Prof. Onora O'Neill

Professor O'Neill is absolutely right, and there is no 'may' about
it. We do have a fundamental obligation, although it is so easily
overlooked in the hurry and stress of daily life. However, one
message that I hope comes through everything I've said is that,

more than anything, the one quality from other people that allows us to be ourselves is simple kindness.

Unkindness is a poisonous dart. Like a stick poked at a hedge-hog, making it curl up to protect itself. So too other people's unkindness, especially from the very people who should love us, makes us draw ourselves in, resulting in a defensive state, sensitive to every perceived slight or wound. As Kahlil Gibran writes, 'Through defending yourself you have finally become full of hate. If you were stronger, you would not use such a weapon.' (4)

Gibran is right; defensiveness can become a weapon and a destructive one. The sad fact is that it begins to develop at a very early age in response to the way we are treated. It seems extraordi-nary, doesn't it, that anyone should have difficulty being kind, especially to their child. Especially to the children in their care, whether in the family, nursery or classroom. Unless, that is, they have been closed off from their kindness by their own wounds. Which is why self-awareness and healing are so important.

I have come to believe that, even before birth, we are a kernel of potential, or 'magnificence' as Diana Cooper would say. The crucial thing is whether or not this 'kernel' is nurtured, encour-aged and empowered, or whether it is dissipated by circumstances over which the developing infant and child have no control. The problem with our potential, our magnificence, being dissipated, is that it takes so much work to get ourselves back together again. It can be the work of a lifetime. At the very least it can take the best part of our lives. Sadly too, we can have hurt those we care about most, before we know we have this work to do, and before the work is completed to a stage that begins to make a difference as to how we are in the world.

MY STORY

As I look back over my life, I see so clearly how the unkindness I experienced turned me in on myself and made me so much less than I could and should have been. I see so clearly too, and was aware even as a child, how the kindness I experienced from certain people allowed me to relax, to breathe more easily, to be a 'nicer' me.

Unfortunately for me, these people were few and far between. Even so, those who were kind are remembered as people who didn't need to score points at my expense, and whose kindness gave me something of immense value. Kindness gives us the strength to hold onto our core self, to retain something of our potential, our magnificence. It also helps to keep hope alive. Hope for something better, for ourselves and those we love. And if we are lucky enough to experience sufficient kindness to retain some belief in ourselves, then an encounter such as I had in my early forties can set us firmly on our healing path.

It was at the end of my first year of counsellor training that our tutor read out the list of essay topics we could choose from. As she read through the list, there was no doubt in my mind which one I should do. The opportunity to concentrate my mind on the experience was one that I could not let pass. The essay title was *A Journey Through Grief* and although grief is usually associated with bereavement there are other ways in which it can be triggered and it was loss rather than death that precipitated my journey through grief. Also, it was only some years later that I came to realise that what I had experienced was in fact the process of grief. To begin with the loss itself would leave so much unexplained, so, to help me make sense of the experience, I looked for and found a letter written five years earlier. I had only read it once in the intervening years, when I had found it quite by 'chance', having thought that it had long since been destroyed. I know now that to write such a letter is in itself a therapeutic exercise. It can provide the first step back from suicide, which indeed it did in my case, and it can be an important part of the healing process.

I started the letter by saying that it might help to talk to someone, but I didn't know who, if anyone, I was talking to. I go on to explain how my mother's rejection of me left me with a gnawing pain which I couldn't escape. I remember hearing an eighty-five-year-old man on the radio crying as he said that all through his life he had lived with the pain of his mother's rejection and I knew just how he felt. I did escape it briefly though, as a mature student, when I attempted to do A levels. I say attempted because I had never done very well at school; I just couldn't apply myself. I remember one geography lesson when I looked out of the window as it started and only 'came back' when what was a double lesson of a subject I liked ended. Looking back I wonder at the teacher not noticing my 'absence'.

However, going back to school at the age of forty I found that in one of the classes I was completely absorbed in the subject. What I also found was that twice a week the pain that had been with me all my life had gone. It wasn't a case of belonging or not belonging, I just was. It wasn't a case of finding an identity at last; it was a case of forgetting myself. Feeling so comfortable, there was a complete lack of awareness of self. I do realise, that for anyone who hasn't lived with the constant pain of rejection, to understand what it was like to feel comfortable after years of discomfort might be difficult. It was like the blissful relief of persistent pain. I purposely didn't count the weeks to the end of the year but watched with anguish as it approached and found that those periods of relief had made the pain feel worse. I decided that suicide was the only solution. I ended the letter by saying: 'So I am going to return to where I came from. To the place I should never have left. But will they be ready for me? Will they be expecting me? Will I again be where I shouldn't be, but this time for eternity? My attempt at escape would be futile. I would be condemning myself to an eternity of rejection. I came into the world uninvited, I mustn't go back uninvited too. I must wait to be called.' At this point I remember my youngest son opening the door of the room where I was writing. It had grown dark and he said, 'Mummy, you're working in the dark.' He put the light on and went out.

Looking back, it was as if a light had come on in my life, and I remember knowing in that moment that suicide would never be an option for me again. Somehow, writing the letter had erased the tapes that had been playing in my mind all my life saying 'You aren't wanted' and 'You don't belong here'. Unbeknown to me, I had begun my journey through grief.

Needing to be occupied, I took another A level the following year, doing a phenomenal amount of work. The philosophy teacher gave us thirty essay questions, suggesting we did as many as we wanted to. I did all of them, getting up at four or five in the morning to get through all the reading. During this year I lost two stones in weight. Food lost its flavour completely. I can remember wondering if I would ever look forward to eating a meal again. My periods stopped and I went into the menopause overnight. My feelings and emotions became numb but my body ached all over. It was a physical effort to get out of bed. I had to drag myself; I seemed to be made of lead. I looked everywhere for the lost teacher; in my mind I was searching constantly.

When my exams were over I realised that I hadn't read an 'ordinary' book for two years, so I went into a bookshop and chose one which the cover said was about a man 'trapped in a twenty-eight year adolescence and fettered to an unexpressed grief'. Even then, I still didn't realise that what I was experiencing was grief. I just thought it might help me and I tried to read it several times that summer but never got beyond the first page.

In October I started at university, but at Christmas my daughter was hurt in a car accident and my dog had to be put down. Either incident on its own would have been traumatic enough, but in addition to these I had carried my grief now for over a year, unable to express how I felt and feeling so alone. When I went back to university after Christmas I couldn't work, nothing was going in, so I asked to intermit. Fortunately I had an understanding advisor and was given permission to do so without having to go into too much detail. I picked up the book I had bought the previous summer and got beyond the first page. It was about a man trying to resolve his grief for his dead mother, which he had carried since he was a young boy. The only comfort or advice he received as a child was from an aunt who told him that what he needed to overcome his grief was inside himself. She said to him, 'You must heal yourself.'

I started back at university the following October and noticed at some point that I was starting to put on weight and that I was no longer searching for the lost teacher, because in some strange way he seemed to have become a part of me. This realisation brought so much comfort with it and gradually I was aware that feelings and emotions were returning and that the lead-like ache had gone. What had also gone was the pain that I had carried all through my life, and the terrible rage which had controlled me was somehow dissipated. I didn't appreciate it then, but know now, that in my grieving for the lost teacher I had done the work of grieving for the loss of my mother's love. In her book, *The Drama of Being a Child*, Alice Miller says that only through grieving our loss can we heal this, the deepest of emotional wounds, that of not being loved and valued for ourselves alone. So that, in retrospect, I see this time of grief, painful as it was, as a gift of healing.

Then on my forty-sixth birthday, while at university, during a lecture on psychopathology, I finally came to understand what had caused the pain that I had carried for so long. What the lecturer said took me back to when I was thirteen, sitting in the wooden armchair between the cooker and the boiler, the warmest place in a very cold house. My mother was standing at the cooker stirring a saucepan. There is no way of knowing what prompted her to say what she did, and it was the nearest I ever heard her come to apologising for making our lives so difficult. She told me that when she knew she was expecting me she was very depressed. She tried very hard to get rid of me, telling me what she'd done. But I wouldn't budge. She said to me, "You were determined to be born." Our life was constantly unhappy. Rows were a daily occurrence and frequently verbal violence would escalate into physical violence. I remember wondering why I had been so determined to be born.

After I was born she didn't want to have anything to do with me. My mother said that for the first two years of my life she had kept me in my cot. 'I just fed and changed you but I never spoke to you or cuddled you.' I was three before she came to terms with the fact that she had another child. She said, 'Wasn't it awful? Do you forgive me?' These were her words, which at the time meant very little to me. It was only when I had my own children that I wondered about those early years and thought that I must have been very lonely.

At the time the implications of this didn't mean anything to me, nor do I think I could have had any real concept of forgiveness. To give her what she wanted was easy and I can remember how pleased I felt to be giving her something that seemed so important to her. At that age, I couldn't possibly have known that not being a wanted baby was the origin of the pain I had carried inside me for as long as I could remember.

However, years later, during that lecture at university it all began to make sense. The lecturer was a tall, impressive figure who was passionate about his subject. He would stride up and down the room asking questions and not pausing long enough for us to answer. He had so much that he wanted to tell us. On this particular morning he was talking about early relationships. He said how important these relationships were and how, if a mother died or was depressed and neglected her baby, it would be like a splinter entering the flesh. As if to emphasise this, he pushed his finger into his arm as he strode towards were I was sitting. As time went on, he said, it would become overlaid, hidden, but it would not lose the power to hurt.

I was stunned. I realised where my pain had originated. For the first time I linked what my mother had told me when I was thirteen to the pain I had carried all my life. The pain that had lived in me, had been part of me, had got so much in the way of life itself, was the effect of her rejection. What I realised too, as I walked out of the lecture, was that Life had waited until that pain had been all but healed before showing me the connection. Of course I can never know how different my life would have been, or the lives of my children, if I had been able to make this connection sooner and been able to consciously seek resolution, rather than it happening unconsciously through a healing encounter, and the work of grief which came in its wake.

GRIEF AS PART OF HEALING

In his book, *A Grief Observed*, C. S. Lewis says, 'What does it matter how this grief of mine evolves or what I do with it?' [5] Well, I know that it matters. What I've learnt from my experience is that grief can be a healing process. Not simply for the loss which caused the grief, but also a process that can heal the pain of past losses, traumas and rejections.

So it matters very much how it evolves, and what we do with it, when something as potentially limiting and painful as loss contains within it so much potential for healing, growth and change. Lewis also says that the changes that take place during the process of grief are 'really not observable. There was no sudden, striking, and emotional transition. Like the warming of a room or the coming of daylight. When you first notice them they have already been going on for some time.' [6]

In this I think he is right. I was not aware of internalisation taking place; it just happened. It was only as I came to learn about grief that I could put a name to it and found that it was a recognised part of the process. Also I couldn't say at what moment the persistent pain I had carried all my life left me. Or at what moment my rage dissipated. One day I just realised they had gone.

In trying to understand this experience, I think that what my teacher possessed was kindness and warmth. They were qualities that were available to all his students, but for me they had a particularly profound effect, especially as they were combined with a positive attitude. In counselling we learn how important it is to prepare the client for the ending of the client/counsellor relationship. Without this, the ending of any relationship can be painful, and experienced as grief.

I think that the moment with my mother when I was thirteen was a very important moment. Although it took till I was forty-six to link her rejection and an unhappy childhood with the internal pain, I did eventually make sense of what the debilitating influence was. We do need to know our history in order to understand ourselves; why and what's going on in our inner world. It is an important part of our healing journey to know this, so we can make sense of feelings that have such a hold over us. In her book, *Lowborn*, a deeply moving account of a chaotic and traumatic childhood, Kerry Hudson has a conversation with a cousin she hasn't spoken to for thirty years. During the conversation the cousin tells her something that no family member has ever told her and which wasn't even to be found in her childhood protection documents. Hearing this truth from her cousin helps her to understand so much about herself.

Strategy for coping with grief:

◆ I'm not sure that we can be aware of internalisation taking place. It is simply a quiet healing that happens on its own.

◆ However, it might help to realise that there are recognised stages to grief that most people experience. They don't necessarily happen in any particular order and the bereaved person can move in and out of the stages as time goes by.

◆ The initial feeling though is usually one of disbelief, followed by numbness. An inexplicable anger can replace the numbness; anger at the loved one for leaving you, followed in time by acceptance of the loss.

◆ This is when internalisation may be experienced, a comforting realisation that you can never really be parted from them, because in some inexplicable way they have become a part of you.

◆ Grief is a deep emotional wound and as with a physical wound you need to attend to what the pain is telling you.

◆ Be gentle with yourself and, if you feel it would help, find someone to talk to, either a trusted friend or a counsellor. Cruse is a wonderful charity which specialises in counselling the bereaved.

◆ Time is your greatest ally: be patient with life and with yourself.

THE SIMPLICITY OF KINDNESS

As for me, I don't think that the legacy of that teacher's kindness will ever end. The work of becoming who we could and should be is never over. But most of all what this experience proves to me is just how important kindness is; it can act as a catalyst for healing and growth. It is one of the most beautiful of human qualities. What that teacher possessed was a rare capacity for kindness. I remember him saying to us that when he was teaching A levels to mature students, he realised that something had stopped us from succeeding first time around, and he didn't want anything to get in the way of our success this time. He never belittled anyone, or tried to score points at the expense of any of his students. Most significantly, I believe that what we all experienced in those classes was consistent kindness and encouragement, which this teacher made available to all his students, hence qualities which were totally unconditional.

Kindness is life enhancing. It conveys both warmth and acceptance. Like love, kindness can be expressed in so many ways, and all of those ways are nurturing. Warmth, which is akin to kindness, is written into Carl Rogers' core conditions as being one of the qualities necessary to begin the work of healing, in a therapeutic relationship. Sadly though, that amounts to shutting the stable door after the horse has bolted, after the wounding has already been done. So much unnecessary emotional distress and damage could be prevented by kindness. It is so simple.

THE IMPORTANCE OF KINDNESS – SUMMARIES

◆ We do have a fundamental obligation to be kind and considerate in our dealings with children.
◆ Unkindness put limits on us.
◆ Defensiveness begins to develop at an early age.
◆ Self-awareness and healing are so important.
◆ Will our kernel of potential, our magnificence, be encouraged or dissipated?
◆ Kindness keeps hope alive.

◆ Writing a letter can be a therapeutic exercise.
◆ In our grieving we also heal other wounds.
◆ The ending of any relationship can be experienced as grief.
◆ Kindness begins the work of healing in a therapeutic relationship.

10

COMPASSIONATE PARENTING

'The parents who have realized their own neglected child within also have drawn forward the inner resources of empathy and compassion to enhance the quality of their relations with their children... The child beneficiaries of such parents will be equipped to meet the difficult challenges of their time, knowing their own true worth and possessing an uninhibited capacity for renewal.'

Jeremiah Abrams

'But I say unto you, "That every idle word that men shall speak, they shall give account thereof in the day of judgement. For by thy words thou shalt be justified And by thy words thou shalt be condemned."'

St. Matthew

We could re-write the second quote to read, 'On the day of judgement we as *parents* will render account' but we must keep in mind the fact that, for us, the day of judgement isn't the day we die. It is every day of our child's life. And every day of our child's life will be a reflection of the impact of our parenting. Every day will bear witness to how we have affected them by the way we have treated them, the quality of our care. Every day we will see the effect of every careless word we have ever uttered; how our *careless* words became indelibly printed on an innocent life. How words, carelessly thrown away by us, have affected the self-esteem of the most important people in our life.

SELF-ESTEEM

The roots of our self-esteem lie in the quality of our early relationships. The words that are spoken over us and to us are already shaping our self-esteem before we even understand their literal meaning. Words are energy, they have impact, and that impact can be constructive or destructive, punitive or nurturing. Even when we need to correct our children, if we are *care full* we can be nurturing and increase their stature, rather than have a debilitating effect on their emerging sense of self. In this way our parenting can be *compassionate parenting* rather than punitive parenting. Just as the food we take in needs to be healthy and nourishing, so too, the words that are directed at us and the impressions we receive should nurture our evolving sense of self.

Just a few years ago I was in a well-known department store, deeply engrossed in a possible purchase. Suddenly from across the store a voice roared out: 'How dare you!' Absorbed as I was in the moment, the force behind this voice sent a wave of pain down my spine. Again it roared: 'How dare you!' I looked to see who the villain was. What I saw was a little boy of about three, strapped in a pushchair, being pushed by a woman who was clearly very put out about something. I thought to myself, what could that little boy possibly have done to warrant such an attack? Because that's what it was, an attack on a defenceless child, because we can hit out as effectively with words as with our fists. And if it caused a pain in my nervous system, what did it do to that little boy's immature nervous system? When we shout at children to relieve something in ourselves, we are causing physical pain, as well as an indelible emotional and psychological scarring.

Many people believe that compassion is something that is desperately needed in our world. The Dalai Lama considers it to be one of the most important of human qualities. He says that compassion is important for mental peace, adding that compassion must be based on respect and a genuine sense of concern for the well-being of another person.

NONVIOLENT COMMUNICATION

This genuine sense of concern for others is behind the work of psychologist Dr. Marshall Rosenberg. He felt so strongly about the importance of the way in which we communicate with one another that he compiled a whole theory on the subject. He calls it Nonviolent Communication, 'a language of compassion', and he bases the concept of NVC on three premises: 'We are simply trying to get our needs met. We fare better if we know how to get these needs met through co-operation rather than aggression. People naturally enjoy contributing to the well-being of others when they can do so willingly.' [3] Rosenberg is passionate about each one of us creating more satisfying connections with each other while also respecting each other's values, which I think emphasises just how important it is to communicate with children at any age, with these three premises in mind.

Rosenberg quotes a fellow American, Andrew Schmookler, as believing that most conflict is caused by attributing 'wrongness' to the other person. We can appreciate how this applies in the wider world, how this attitude fuels conflict and war. But it also applies to a great extent between parent and child. So often the motives of children are misunderstood by a parent or parents who are preoccupied with other things.

I am reminded of a little girl whose mother wasn't very well and their normally immaculate house was looking a little sad. The little girl offered to do some tidying and the mother asked why. The little girl said because the house was looking untidy which the mother experienced as a criticism and told the child off. This all ended with the child in tears, and what had she learnt? That to offer to help and to speak the truth could get her into trouble. Sadly it is so easy for an adult to misinterpret the intentions of a child. Reason tells us that to project an adult perspective onto what a child does is unreasonable but it's easily done in the heat of the moment, especially if we are feeling unwell or worrying about something.

DE-PROGRAMMING

Parents have all the power. What they say goes. If we had parents who expected to be obeyed to the letter, chances are we would be the same. As parents it is our turn to lay the law down. I remember that, when my eldest son was about seven and I would ask him to do something, invariably he would do it differently from how I'd asked. This used to make me cross. He should do as he was told. 'Do as I say.' I can hear my mother saying this as I write. Then I realised that when I asked him to do something and he did it differently from how I'd asked, it was because he could see a *better* way of doing it. He is very practical, and has a gift for seeing a quick and sure way to do things. There is no way of knowing just how much frustration and damage I caused (because I'd been programmed into thinking that parents were always right and I was a parent now), before I realised that I wasn't always right, and, more importantly, that I didn't have to be.

> *'I've never seen a stupid kid;*
> *I've seen a kid who sometimes did*
> *things I didn't understand*
> *or things in ways I hadn't planned;*
> *I've seen a kid who hadn't seen*
> *the same places where I have been,*
> *but he was not a stupid kid. Before you call*
> *him stupid,*
> *think, was he a stupid kid or did he just*
> *know different things than you did?'*

Ruth Bebermeyer [4]

COMPASSIONATE CARE

In his book, *Mental Health Nursing – The Art of Compassionate Care*, Peter Watkins says in the introduction that he has come to believe strongly in compassionate care as the 'mainspring' of recovery. And I'm sure that he is right. I am equally sure that a compassionate approach to parenting, if it became the norm, would eliminate an enormous amount of psychological and therefore emotional and mental pain.

Reflecting on what he calls anti-oppressive approaches to mental health nursing, two of the points he makes have important implications for parenting. The questions that mental health nurses should ask themselves are relevant questions for parents to ask themselves. For instance it is important for them to take into consideration the environmental factors that are a contributing factor in a person's mental distress. This translates into parents being aware that temper tantrums, in infancy or adolescence, or at any time, are expressions of distress which are, at least in part, a product of the social, cultural and parental influences over which *the child has had no control.* Also, if nurses should relate to patients in a way that empowers them and nurtures their self-esteem, how much more should we as parents and carers remember to relate in this way to the child in our care?

Peter Watkins also reflects on the qualities needed for compassionate intervention in times of client crisis. He talks about intervening in a way that contributes a sense of safety and containment, so reducing the level of stress for everyone (shades of Carl Rogers' person-centred approach). This is relevant when interacting with children at any stage of their development. It's also important for us to remain calm and listen, to be undemanding and compassionate, so anchoring the patient (child) in calmer psychological waters. Just those words – calmer psychological waters – have a deeply healing energy.

I love his book for the compassionate approach that it advocates for the care of psychologically distressed people and, by extension, its relevance to parenting. He describes the process of recovery as a means to truly come to know ourselves and discover who we really are. This is also the process at the heart of counselling both for ourselves when we are training and in the work we do with clients. He adds that it is about finding the 'beautiful' self at the heart of each of us. The beautiful self that has been overlaid by life, by other people's wounds, inadequacy or unkindness.

PHYSICAL HARM

I remember receiving a letter from the NSPCC Green Dot campaign asking me if I would support legislation to give children the same protection from being hit that we adults expect. The answer is a resounding *YES*. The letter goes on to say 'Many of us were taught that physical punishment is necessary for bringing up well-behaved children.' But I think it is also true to say that we learnt as children that parents are entitled to get their own way quickly, by hitting us. Thereby they showed us that they had an *awful* power that they were prepared to use. Not only did many of us come to understand that as children, but if we were hit we probably thought it was *okay* to hit our own children.

As children, we lived permanently on the receiving end of our mother's unhappiness which manifested by turn as anger, depression and, I would say at times, hate. It was a very uncomfortable place to be. As a parent I thought I was lenient compared to the way in which I had been treated as a child. I did love my children and I'm not sure that my mother was capable of love. But even my love for them couldn't protect them from the terrible rage that my childhood had left in me. So that, despite being a loving mother in many ways, I had what would be described as a short fuse, and could hit out physically and verbally in a way that I deeply regret now. Which is why I wish legislation had been in place when they were young. If it had been, despite my experiences as a child, my *programming* would have had to find another way, and then at least the cycle of physical punishment would have been broken.

The breaking of that cycle has had to wait for another generation to be put in place and it is so good to know that today the right for parents and any authority figure to use physical punishment is all but over. As it was, I didn't have the incentive of the law and it took me years of hard, conscious effort to change my programming. I mentioned in an earlier chapter the moment when an awareness of what I was doing and the need to change was brought home to me. That moment of awareness was the beginning of my journey, and it has been a long one. Some of which I've shared, partly to show just how much of a lifetime needs to be spent retrieving our lost selves, and partly to show that it can be done. Sadly, in some respects it was too late, my unhappy childhood had got in the way of the mother I could have been and at times had made life more difficult for my beautiful children than it needed to have been.

However, I am grateful that seeing the need to change lessened the damage that might have been done. Even so, to realise how deeply ingrained our programming is, how difficult it is to change, even when it is what you want, makes me realise how important it is that this unnecessary wounding doesn't happen in the first place.

The 'beautiful self' that Peter Watkins talks about shouldn't be lost to us because of a lack of awareness in others. The theologian W. E. Sangster described kindness as a universal language that can be understood by everyone. He said it that it allows people to hope again. But how does hope get lost? If we paid more attention to the way children are treated in the home, at school and by the media, barriers wouldn't need to go up and hope wouldn't get lost. We also need to be honest with ourselves about the way in which we were treated by our parents and the effect it has had on us. That is to say the way it has impacted us emotionally and the legacy of that impact. We must be ready and willing to own and work on our wounds, if not simply for ourselves but also for our children because 'The quality and success of parenting is deeply enhanced when parents can realise their own neglected child selves and transform them into compassionate resources for the care of their own children. *The way one treats the inner child strongly determines the way one treats the outer child.*' (5)

OUR INNER CHILD

Our inner child and his/her impact on our life is poignantly evoked by Kerry Hudson in her book *Lowborn*. She describes reading her child protection documents and from the safety of a 'comfortable' adult life wonders incomprehensibly at the lack of intervention from social services. She wants to have some compassion for those involved in the decision making which left her so vulnerable, adding, 'But then there was that child. And I realised my childhood made itself known to me every single day. In the way I engaged with others, when I slept, when and what I ate. In the thought patterns seemingly designed to undermine me, to make me feel beneath whoever I was interacting with, which made me beg in all sorts of ways for their approval. In the deep loneliness, the way I often said I was a "black hole for love", no matter how much I had been and was loved in my adult life.' [6]

These words are deeply moving. They were once true for me as they still are for so many people. All through my work with clients I was very aware of contacting and working with their inner child. The child they once were, the child they carried. This wasn't difficult because, as I've said before, it is the deep-seated unhappy experiences in childhood that bring most people into counselling and the child they once were soon comes into the room. As these childhood experiences are contacted I am a witness to what was experienced. This, coupled with the fact that in some alchemical way the client is no longer alone with the experience, can be the beginning of their healing journey. I have mentioned before about being our own best mother and here we can extend this notion, if necessary, to being our own best parents.

INTEGRATING OUR YOUNG SELF

This inner child, who Jung believed was relevant not only to our past but to our present and future life, is said to connect us to the joy and sadness of our childhood. Where someone has had more joy than sorrow they are luckier than they will ever know. However, for those of us for whom childhood sadness far outweighed the joy, there is important work to do. If we ignore or reject our child self – the self where all the emotions that we couldn't express are locked – we remain fragmented and, since this child is said to be the most vital and spontaneous part of ourselves, it is crucially important to consciously integrate this aspect of the self into our life so we can become whole.

Strategies for integrating the inner child:

- Accept that we all carry an inner child who has been with us from the beginning.
- Acknowledge the presence of your inner child.
- Looking at photos of yourself as a young child can help you to connect with this child.
- Be protective and feel love and compassion for your young self.
- Imagine this little child being with you and welcome him or her into your life now.
- It may help to talk to someone. This way you have a witness and you and your inner child are no longer alone with what you experienced.
- Some of you may find *Running From Safety* by Richard Bach an interesting perspective on the wisdom of our inner child.

Very often having a witness to childhood injustices, acknowledging the wounds, saying it wasn't okay to be treated in such a way, can begin the healing journey of integration. Some people like to carry a photo of themselves as a child or they imagine their inner child as being with them and loving and taking care of them. If we listen to our inner child with what Buddhists call self-compassion, naming our needs for healing and fulfilment and by extension listening to ourselves too, the compassion we feel for ourselves can, paradoxically, help us to become more compassionate parents.

The more we can bring compassion to our parenting the more we will build and strengthen our children's self-esteem. This is arguably the most important facet of their human beingness, contributing, as it does, to the resilience and well-being they will need as they go out into the world. And this is so important because, as the philosopher C. D. McGee reminded us in his book *The Recovery of Meaning*, there comes a time when we have to let our children go out into the world on their own. The price the world will exact from them, as McGee says, and we know, is their precious innocence. There is nothing we can do about this. There isn't any way that we can renegotiate this price with the world. All we can do is to ensure their 'good beginning'; that alone is down to us. We must do all in our power to ensure they have the foundation, the inner strength and the self-esteem, to meet this world and everything it demands of them.

COMPASSIONATE PARENTING – SUMMARIES

◆ Careless words can become indelibly printed on an innocent life.
◆ The roots of our self-esteem lie in the quality of our early relationships.
◆ Words are energy which can be nurturing or punitive.
◆ Children thrive on compassionate nurture.
◆ We can hit out as effectively with our words as with our fists.
◆ Compassion is desperately needed in our world.
◆ Nonviolent Communication is a language of compassion.
◆ We mustn't project our adult perspective onto the intentions of a child.
◆ Compassionate care is the most important aspect of recovery.
◆ The importance of being a compassionate presence.
◆ Physical punishment towards children is not okay.

◆ It's hard to change our deeply ingrained programming.

◆ Regaining the 'beautiful self' at the heart of each of us.

◆ Importance of working with the inner child.

◆ A child's self-esteem contributes to their resilience and well-being as they meet the challenges of life.

11

ADOLESCENCE

'*The most common cause of disability among teenagers is mental illness. Symptoms of depression, whether major or minor, affect up to one third of teenagers…*'

Daniel Goleman

Adolescence is a crucial stage in our development since it is when the second major attempt at individuation takes place. It is a time when our true self will try once more to do the work of what I think of as *primary individuation*, the attempt of the toddler to find his/her place in the world, which, first time around, was either prevented or impaired by circumstances, in whatever shape or form.

ERIKSON'S STAGES OF DEVELOPMENT

This brings to mind the contribution of Erikson's stages of development which I mentioned in earlier chapters. What I didn't say though, which is important to include, is that the completion of each task results in an ego or what I'd prefer to call an inner strength, which is equally important for individual well-being. So for instance, where we saw in the first stage that the task for the 0–1-year-old was 'trust versus mistrust', the inner strength to be achieved is hope and we know how important and potent hope is for us throughout life.

In the next stage, 1–3 years, the years of infancy, the task is 'autonomy versus shame and doubt'. Here the inner strength to be achieved is will, which highlights how important it is to constructively resolve those tantrums.

What we haven't yet touched on are the third through to the fifth stages. In the third stage, the young child from 3–5 years faces the task of 'initiative versus guilt', the inner strength being purpose. In stage four, the school-aged child (5–12 years) faces the task of 'industry versus inferiority' with the inner strength being competence. Stage five, the last stage of childhood, is when tasks not satisfactorily completed in earlier stages will come to the fore again, seeking resolution. This is adolescence, from 12–18 years, where the task is 'identity versus role confusion' and the inner strength is loyalty.

Now of course this is simply a theory, put forward by Erikson as a guide to what a child may need to accomplish in the formative years. No stage is fixed: the stages are fluid and what isn't achieved in one stage can be resolved a bit further down the line. However, it is a helpful guide and one that is worth having in mind as we consider what is possibly going on for children in their adolescent years. What we also need to bear in mind is puberty at this stage and what that entails in terms of the bodily changes that accompany puberty, changes which the child cannot opt out of and which may be welcomed or possibly viewed with anxiety and the roller-coaster of emotions that the unknown brings with it.

We can think of adolescence as a time when the tasks of previous stages which, for whatever reason, were not successfully or satisfactorily completed will reassert themselves and ideally be given an opportunity to find resolution. So it is important that problems arising at this time are taken seriously, in the hope that they can indeed be resolved at this stage in the child's life and not left to cause problems later on.

SELF-REFLECTION

Therapists who write about working with troubled adolescents appear to agree on one fundamental issue: the crucial need in the adolescent for the capacity to self-reflect. That is, to have the capacity to think about how they feel, why they feel the way they do and how best to cope with those feelings. The capacity for self-reflection allows emotions to be contained, controlled, channelled and understood. Without self-reflection emotions can be overwhelming and out of control, possibly leading to violence or self-harm.

When I had been married just a short time, I realised that I was never lost in thought. My mind was either totally taken up with what I was doing in the present moment or it was dwelling miserably and destructively on the past. Of course I didn't know then that what I lacked was the capacity for self-reflection but that's what it was. And it isn't a good place to be, because, once you start down the road of past misery and hurts, emotions and the pain that accompanies them can build up inside you until only an act of violence brings relief. During the first few years of my marriage, I smashed my way through a whole set of china. Looking back I hardly recognise myself and realise what a shock it must have been for my husband and for my young son who would have watched me do some of the smashing, just as I had witnessed emotions getting out of control in my troubled family when I was growing up.

So I know from bitter experience just how important the capacity for self-reflection is, and how destructive we can be to ourselves and others, if the circumstances of infancy and childhood have prevented this capacity from developing. Because it is the 'circumstances of infancy and childhood' that have prevented it. Moses Lauffer, writing about adolescents in therapy, says that if the therapist mishandles the therapy it could result in long-term detrimental effects for the adolescent. In just the same way, 'mishandling' in infancy and childhood can have a long-term detrimental effect on a child's adolescent and adult life.

At an unconscious level, this might be the work an adolescent child is trying to accomplish, which is why at this stage of their lives they are often described as being narcissistic; it requires a self-absorption that can be misunderstood by those around them. It is also why it is so important to try and find out what exactly lies behind what may appear to be antisocial or simply difficult behaviour.

When we hear the term 'young offender', we may automatically associate it with aggressive, uncontrollable behaviour. Understandably this opens up a void between them and us; them and society. But if we accept what Rosenberg says, that 'at the core of all anger is a need that is not being fulfilled', (2) and if we think of this behaviour as the only language they can use to give expression to their inner turmoil and pain, (shades of the tantrums associated with the terrific twos), then compassion and the need to resolve this for them (and for society) will motivate us to bridge that void and identify and resolve what's going on for them, before it gets carried on into adult life and causes even more damage to themselves and others.

So what qualities does a therapist need to make available, in order to help a young person who hasn't, as yet, had the opportunity to develop the capacity for self-reflection? In other words, what conditions would parents need to provide in infancy and childhood that would have allowed this crucial capacity to develop?

Most importantly, the therapist offers the troubled adolescent ongoing and consistent support and help. It is an important part of the healing process that the adolescent experiences that support and helpfulness as being totally available to him, to his inner 'self'; as being there because 'he/she' matters. What the therapist builds, and what the adolescent needs to experience, is a relationship of trust; a dependable relationship based on mutual respect, where his/her ultimate good is of paramount importance.

Breathtakingly simple, and what every infant should 'enjoy' as a birthright: a parent who is there for them, supportive and helpful; a parent who wants to 'understand' their child, what their child needs; a parent *whose own needs don't get in the way* of their love for their infant child, for the adult in the making, and the quality of life their child will experience for the rest of their life.

The most crucial input from the therapist is to have and show an interest in the adolescent, for their own sake. To show the child (because that is what an adolescent is) that they themselves are not the problem, but that they are carrying a problem which has been put 'onto' them. With this established, the therapist and adolescent are able to collaborate in finding out what or who the problem is, and begin the work of relieving the child of this burden.

'PROBLEM' CHILDREN

I often hear people say that so-and-so's child is a problem. I want to say that the child is not the problem, but that they are, without doubt, 'carrying' a problem for someone else or perhaps even a whole family. A problem which is not of their making has been taken out on them, or put onto them, and the behaviour that manifests through them becomes a distraction from the real problem. This problem can often be deeply rooted in a family and may have been passed from generation to generation. Sadly, scapegoating in families isn't as uncommon as we might hope and, if a child is made to feel bad, this in itself can become a self-fulfilling prophecy.

I remember hearing about a young adolescent boy who had been in therapy for several years. He said that his mother was 'always getting on at him'. She said that on occasion he had lashed out at her and that she was afraid of him. He had now been excluded from therapy, his only possible hope, because he had hit out at his therapist. To me he sounded like a very frustrated and unhappy young boy, who no one was listening to. How could they expect him to improve, when they kept returning him to the situation that had caused the problem in the first place? How could he change, when nothing was done to find out why the mother needed to keep 'getting on' at him? It amounted to pluck-ing a drowning child from a raging sea, resuscitating him, and then throwing him back. Something needed to be done about the circumstances he was going back to and coping with. The mother needed help to become aware of her contribution to his behav-iour, and should have received support to address the problems in her life which led to her nagging him. Anyone who hasn't lived with someone who nags cannot be expected to understand how mind-bending it is. In fact, nagging can drive you to distraction, and make you agree to almost anything to be free of the mental torment of the nagging.

My mother was someone who relieved her own internal distress by nagging. She would get on at us until we complied with her unreasonable demands. Paulo Coelho perceptively writes, 'Some people always have to be doing battle with someone. Sometimes even with themselves, battling with their own lives. So they begin to create a kind of play in their head, and they write the script based on their frustrations… But the worst part is that they cannot present the play themselves… so they begin to invite other actors to join in.' [3]

As children we don't have much choice about the plays our parents want to direct. In our family we were all unwillingly drawn into my mother's unhappy, destructive plays. But it was my brother who suffered the most. He was the scapegoat for her unhappy childhood and loveless marriage. Our mother would get on at him until I could hardly bear it myself. Sometimes he would lash out at her in a desperate attempt to stop the tirade, and she responded as if that was exactly what she had wanted. The line between hitting out to stop the nagging, and actually doing some physical harm, must have been a very fine one, and if my brother had done my mother physical harm, the finger of blame would have been pointed at him. In the eyes of society, he would have been the one at fault, the one with the 'problem'. And he did indeed have a problem, in that our mother constantly took out her own hurt, anger and frustration on him. Yet the truth was that my mother, damaged by her own childhood, was the one at 'fault'.

The one who set the agenda and needed help. Driven by some uncontrollable force inside her, it must have been her way of gaining some relief.

RELEASING THE BURDEN

To say that the adolescent is the problem is to compound the damage, the injustice, that has already been done. It is to collude with everything that has control over the child, but over which the child has no control. Instead of dealing with a problem child, we should identify the problem that the child is carrying, the burden that has been, for whatever reason, placed on them by someone who has power over them. Only by doing this, can the child be released from this burden and lead the life that is truly theirs.

Strategy: Identifying and releasing the burden for the child:

◆ Gaining the trust of the child will be the first and crucial step for the counsellor or concerned adult.
◆ Gently encourage the child to talk about what is troubling them.
◆ Find where or with whom the problem originates.
◆ Let the child know that they are not the problem.
◆ Find ways to treat the problem at its source with appropriate help in whatever way is needed.
◆ Provide empathic support for the child while they heal from all the implications of having carried this burden which they weren't responsible for.

We talk about 'disturbed' children and forget that they weren't born disturbed. They have been 'disturbed' by a world that has failed them. However, with an awareness of what we are doing on everyone's part, most mishandling needn't happen and those mistakes we do inevitably make won't have such an impact. If a child has been lucky, then adolescence will be a time when the world with all its possibilities is opening up for them, offering the opportunity to explore what's right for them. In the best of all possible worlds, they will discover a true balance between mind, body, self-acceptance and, above all, emotional well-being.

ADOLESCENCE – SUMMARIES

◆ Second major attempt at individuation will take place.

◆ Erikson's stages of development.

◆ Adolescence is the last stage of childhood when tasks not completed earlier seek resolution.

◆ Problems arising at this time must be taken seriously.

◆ There is a crucial need for an adolescent to have the capacity to self-reflect.

◆ Narcissism and self-absorption may be important for some adolescents to enable them to focus on resolving earlier tasks.

◆ Important to find out what lies behind antisocial or difficult behaviour.

◆ Look behind the anger for the need which is not being met.

◆ The therapist makes available ongoing and consistent support and help.

◆ This help and support are available to the adolescent because he/she matters.

◆ Our needs must not get in the way of our children's.

◆ The adolescent isn't the problem; he/she is carrying a problem of someone else's making.
◆ Children are drawn into their parents' scripts.
◆ Identify the problem the child is carrying.
◆ Children are not born disturbed.

12

SELF-AWARENESS
The Key to Fulfilment

'First know thyself.'

Oracle at Delphi

'... far more frequently troubles seem to arise because parents themselves have emotional difficulties of which they are only partially aware and which they cannot control.'

Bowlby

'The first step towards personal freedom is awareness. We need to be aware that we are not free in order to be free. We need to be aware of what the problem is in order to solve the problem. Awareness is always the first step because if you are not aware, there is nothing you can change.'

Ruiz

All through our training as counsellors we are taught that genuineness on the part of the counsellor is a vital part of a successful therapeutic relationship. There is no healing or growth without it. But how do we become 'genuine' after a lifetime's adaptation to the demands of life? Reflecting on the 'problem' of being human, Barry Stevens says, 'In the beginning was I, and I was good. Then came in other I. Outside authority. This was confusing. And then other I became very confused because there were so many different outside authorities. Sit nicely. Leave the room to blow your nose… Flush the toilet at night… Don't flush the toilet at night, you wake people up! Always be nice to people. Even if you don't like them, you mustn't hurt their feelings. Be frank and honest. If you don't tell people what you think of them, that's cowardly… The most important thing is to have a career. The most important thing is to get married… The most important thing is to have money in the bank. The most important thing is to have everyone like you. The most important thing is to dress well. The most important thing is to be sophisticated and say what you don't mean and don't let anyone know what you feel… And others say all these things… I gets lost…' [3]

Here, Barry Stevens captures the bewilderment which starts in childhood and makes it clear that knowing who we are, after a lifetime of conformity, is far from easy. As she said, *'In the beginning was I, and I was good.'* But then inevitably all the injunctions come to us from every possible direction. And these days those injunctions are ubiquitous; they come, particularly via the media, for every conceivable reason.

As the Oracle said, 'First know thyself.' Self-awareness is the key, and the key to self-awareness is the willingness to explore the inner self with an open heart, to see how and why we respond to life's situations in the way we do. I've mentioned before how the day when I was shouting at my children proved to be a turning point for me. Although I didn't realise it at the time, it was an important moment of self-awareness. What I didn't realise either was that I had a mountain of repressed emotions inside me that seemingly only anger could relieve. Even so, the still small voice, which is so often drowned out, on this occasion made itself heard and I became aware of what I was doing and knew I had to change. But knowing that we *need* to change, and knowing *how* to change, are not mutually inclusive.

I was very lucky that the still small voice made itself heard. The repercussions for children when parents take their frustrations out on them are far-reaching. What little I know of my grandmother leaves me in no doubt that she was a wounded, wounding woman. This, of course, was not solely of her making, but her treatment of my mother, for whatever reason, rendered my mother capable of great unkindness to her own children. We children, who were totally innocent of doing any harm to her, nevertheless lived on the end of her woundedness, her formidable anger. Not a good place to find yourself in, or to go out into the world from. It was a crippling place, and, as much as I tried to be different from her, she was my role model, she had programmed me, and inevitably some of her wounding wounded me and sadly some was passed on to my beautiful children.

SAFETY AND EQUILIBRIUM

One of the most important tasks that a parent has to do is to teach their children to get back from any upsetting experience to a place of safety and equilibrium. The parent does this by comforting the child when things go wrong or when they are hurt, offering reassurance and getting their world back onto an even keel. But if no one ever did this for the parent, if a parent is preoccupied with their own feelings or has difficulty in coping with them, their children will suffer. They won't be able to respond adequately to the needs of their baby or may not even be aware of what those emotional needs are. Not only that but an important aspect of relationships with others is dependent on our being able to read the other person's feelings. If we can't cope with our own, we aren't in a position to understand where someone else is coming from.

So I know, from what has been passed down through my own experience of three generations, that self-awareness is crucial. Self-awareness, being aware of our impact on other people's lives, particularly our children's, can help to moderate the detrimental and powerful effects early experiences can have on the way we behave. It is only through becoming self-aware, understanding ourselves, how and why our emotions work, and our own psychological make-up, that we can be in charge of our own lives, and be *there* in a meaningful way for our own children. It is only from this vantage point that we can make something secure and sustaining, available to our children as they go through life's inevitable challenges.

WALKING WOUNDED

Unfortunately many of us are not secure. Outwardly adult, we carry within us a wounded child, whose very presence in our psychological make-up is a limiting and crippling influence. This was poignantly brought home to me by a client who I had been seeing for some weeks, who I felt great empathy and warmth for. One day I came out of a session, feeling as though I had been in a battle. I can remember how perplexed I was by this feeling. After all, to be in a battle implied that we were on different sides. But we weren't; I was there for her, so I needed to know just what was going on. When I saw her again, I said that I had come out of the previous session feeling as though I had been in a battle and that I couldn't understand it, because we were on the same side. She asked me whose side I was on and I replied that of course I was on her side. "In that case," she said, "we aren't on the same side." By which she meant that *she* wasn't on her side. She went on to explain that, as a child, her parents were always criticising her. It seemed that she couldn't do anything right. They were always looking over her shoulder criticising everything she did and they were still there, looking over her shoulder and finding fault. Sadly, at some point she had joined them. So it wasn't only her parents who stood looking over her shoulder and criticising her, she was there too!

I remember that I felt real shock and sadness at the image she was living with, and at how deeply ingrained it was. And yet I have come to realise that many of us do exactly this to ourselves. Most of us have internalised a critical voice. Very often it is the voice of a parent or teacher, or other authority figure. Someone who has been in a position of power, whose treatment of us has left a lasting, wounding impression on our psyche. This wounding of the psyche is subtle and insidious. Because it is on the psyche, it is both part of us, and a very influential part, but also set to one side of our immediate awareness. Whereas if it were an obvious wound, we would attend to it until it was healed.

I do wonder if this client's experience resonates for you. You might like to ask yourself if you are aware of a critical internal voice and where it might have originated? A parent, carer, teacher, or someone you admired who didn't deserve your admiration? If you can identify the perpetrator it will go a long way towards relinquishing their hold on you and you may eventually silence them altogether.

As this client's experience illustrates, not only do we internalise critical authority voices, we also dutifully carry on their work, by adding our own voice to the chorus. The voice of our wounded and so wounding child. Part of the work of becoming self-aware is to contact this inner child, and Paulo Coelho, in his book *By The River Piedra I Sat down and Wept*, emphasises the need to pay attention to our inner child, what he calls the 'child in our heart', because befriending this child, the child we once were, can help us get back to who we could and should be, our core self, our original birthright, our potential. But it is also important to befriend our inner child so that he or she no longer has to make their presence felt, by getting in the way of our adult self and tripping up the relationships we could and should be having, not only with partners and friends but most importantly with the children we bring into our world.

MAGNIFICENCE

In her book *A Little Light on the Spiritual Laws*, Diana Cooper echoes the words of psychiatrist Dr. Brian Weiss when she says, 'If you constantly criticise or find fault with a child, you will never know his magnificence.' [4] This is so true. Many people are cut off from their magnificence. To be cut off from your magnificence, your potential, is a tragedy and we have to work hard if we want to regain even a semblance of it. Seeing your own child cut off from his or her magnificence is an even greater tragedy. One way of avoiding this harm to our children is to understand ourselves: what motivates us and why we react the way we do in any given circumstance. We may think we know, but very often we don't. Perhaps Sara's story can best describe what I mean.

Sara was an attractive woman in her forties. She cried and talked all through the first session. When she left she said she would see me again the following week but I didn't expect to see her because I hadn't felt that I had made 'contact' with her. I had simply received this outpouring, this deluge of grief. However, she did come to the session the following week and said that she realised that she had told me something which had happened to her years ago, which she hadn't ever told anyone. She said that the feelings around what had happened were so overwhelming that, although she had tried to forget the incident, she now realised that these feelings had been getting in her way all these years.

I told her that an important part of the counselling process was to bring together events and feelings so that we understand where certain feelings come from and so begin the work of healing. She had found this out very early in counselling, but it was a discovery most people made later on. Sara said that she knew exactly what I meant. Until a few years ago, a certain perfume made her feel like crying and she hated it. Then, a couple of years ago, she was in a department store with her mother when an assistant sprayed some into the air near where they were standing. She told her mother that she hated the perfume. Her mother was surprised, saying that it was the perfume she used to wear when Sara was a little girl, when she and her husband went out for the evening. Sara immediately realised why it made her want to cry. She had always been unhappy when they left. Despite the presence of the babysitter, she would feel so alone, perhaps fearing, as a child might, that they would never come back. Sara said that once she had made the connection between the perfume and those childhood memories, she no longer felt like crying when she smelt the perfume, although she still didn't like it!

The point is that she now knew *why* she felt as she did when she smelt the perfume. Knowing this released her from the sadness (sadness that had its roots in fear and so was very powerful) that had remained locked inside her since she was a little girl. It was such a clear example that I asked her permission to use it when I wanted to explain how counselling works. Similarly, talking about the trauma from years ago helped her to realise where overwhelming feelings were coming from and so begin the work of healing.

Finding out what makes us sad, what gets in the way of our most important relationships and all relationships, down to the merest encounter, in short, what is parting us from our 'magnificence', is without doubt the most important work we will ever do. We need to attend to what's happening inside, to what's happening in our external world, and to our responses. Is the internal response the same as the external one, and is it the response that we want to make? If it isn't, how can we change it to the one we do want?

SELF-OBSERVATION

Anthony De Mello, in his book *Awareness*, says that an open, attentive attitude brings change effortlessly and I'm sure he is right. For many of us though, reaching a place where we can maintain an open, attentive attitude isn't easy, but it is worth the effort. Understanding ourselves requires sustained self-observation, which De

Mello says is not the same as self-absorption. We need to understand ourselves and accept ourselves and we don't achieve this overnight; it is a step-by-step process.

A fundamental part of training as a counsellor is about understanding ourselves, what makes us tick, or not tick, as the case may be. It was early in my training that I came to understand meaningfully something I had carried and was still carrying, which frequently tripped me up. I was at a workshop on Transactional Analysis where we were asked to write down the predominant message that we received as children, from our parents and birth family. I remember hearing in my mind what I had been told so often as a child, and still was told as a 'joke' in my adult life. I remember staring at the blank page, wondering if I could write the words down. Eventually I did write them and confronted the words on the page and the feelings those words invoked inside me. What I had written and what I read was, 'You weren't invited.' It was a phrase frequently used, which, as a young child, told me that what I wanted or what I'd done didn't count, was of little or no value.

We were asked to look at what we had written and to try to evaluate the effect that it had had on us – how it made us feel, and how those feelings manifested in our lives. We had to ask ourselves what, if any, influence it might still be exerting on us. I knew that it had always felt, and still felt, very dismissive of everything that I was. What I hadn't realised though, until we were asked to think about it, was just how far-reaching that effect was. I knew that even now, when I was invited somewhere I never felt 'welcome.' It was a feeling that permeated everything I did. I had nearly reached the end of my forties and this family message was still undermining my confidence, my whole life.

Understanding what was happening doesn't solve the problem straightaway; we have to work at it. Gradually, I came to realise that, even if as a child I hadn't been 'invited', and my presence in the family had caused additional difficulties in an already unhappy household, as an adult nobody had to 'invite' me to anything where they didn't really want me. When I was invited somewhere, it was most probably because I was actually welcome. Now there is no longer the dread that had always accompanied social events. Definitely a case of better late than never, and it illustrates how understanding ourselves can release us from the limits that other people have put onto us, and which we, very often, unwittingly perpetuate. 'What you are aware of you are in control of; what you are not aware of is in control of you. You are always a slave to what you're not aware of.' (5)

Transactional Analysis showed me something that was important for me, something that was well worth knowing and understanding. You could try this exercise for yourself – you don't have to go to a workshop on TA to ask yourself the question: 'What was the predominant message I received as a child from my parents and family?' If you are lucky the message you received was that you were loved and valued. However, if you received a negative message you might need to look at how it could still be impacting your life. Realising that the message was about them and not you can begin the healing process and free you from its negative influence.

Strategies for coping when the message is a negative one could be:

- Remember that this is about them; it isn't about you.
- However, it will have impacted your life.

- It will take a certain amount of courage to look at what was said and how you feel.
- Knowing what these are, you will need to consider whether or not you are happy with the ways in which they manifest in your behaviour and reactions.
- This is work you can do on your own or perhaps a few sessions with a counsellor could help you explore possible options.
- You owe it to yourself to do this and release your beautiful self from the limits that others have put on you.

It is probably true to say that all of us, to some extent, are living with impediments to our potential and to our happiness. Giving ourselves the opportunity to find out what they are and work on eliminating them from our lives is an important step towards loving and valuing ourselves and this in itself can have important implications for us as parents. This is because, at some level, we will experience our children as an extension of ourselves, so that if we don't love and accept ourselves, it is easier to treat them in the same harsh ways that we were once treated.

Simply put, if we want to be self-aware and improve our quality of life, we need to bring insight and understanding to our wounds and the conflicts they create inside ourselves. This will ensure that we don't take these conflicts out on other people, most importantly our children, at such a cost and loss to everyone involved. These days there is an abundance of self-help books to choose from, covering just about every area of our lives. Importantly they are holistic, that is to say they will speak to your mind, heart and soul; no part of you is left out. Or it might be helpful to go to self-awareness workshops or courses, or to sit down with a counsellor to explore your life and find out what is going on. This isn't the big deal it might once have been. In fact you could say that you owe it to yourself and your children to do it. If there are issues that are taking control of your life away from you, it's important to do something about it. If you don't, your children will have a harder time than they deserve, and may need help themselves later in life.

SELF-ESTEEM

Inextricably linked to self-awareness is the issue of self-esteem. 'As children, many of us were forced to suppress our power because the adults around us didn't want competition. *They* wanted to be powerful and demanded that we be weak so we wouldn't threaten them. All that power is still there, hidden, waiting for us to tap it and use it in our lives.' [6] And tap into it we must if we are to live our lives the way we could and should in order to even begin to fulfil our potential. In her book, *Anatomy of the Spirit*, Caroline Myss says that this lack of self-esteem robs us of everything. And she's right: it's another of those vicious circles that it is imperative to become aware of and change. Fortunately, we can do something about our situation and she provides suggestions as to how we might go about changing the conditioned way we view ourselves. So briefly, what does each stage of regaining our innate power require from us?

Nothing less than a revolution is needed by those of us (and we are legion) who have been conditioned, from the very beginning of our lives, to 'do as we are told'. To toe the line in the family home is to toe the line socially. If you are put down in the home, chances are you will be put down, overtly and covertly, in the outside world. It is another of those vicious circles, from which it is so difficult to escape. But escape we must if we are to have any sort of a life. Socrates said that the unexamined life isn't worth living but nor is a life which is at the beck and call of everyone but yourself. So, nothing less than a revolution is necessary. It doesn't have to be big. Lots of little revolutions will do, to help you gradually acquire the courage of your convictions and stand by what you know is right for you, even in the face of opposition.

Gaining courage in this way, on the outside of our lives, goes hand in hand with gaining courage to look within. This type of looking within isn't done in a critical way; it is done in a spirit of enquiry. We are giving ourselves the chance to find our own truth and to listen to the voice within, which in the past has been drowned out by other people's injunctions. This period of involution is followed by narcissism, similar to the crucially important stage of narcissism in adolescence. Chances are that you didn't get a good innings at narcissism as an adolescent, which is why giving yourself the opportunity now is so important.

It might be helpful in this crucial stage of narcissism – in the recreating of yourself – to think about the things you don't like about yourself and your life and then think about what you do like about your life and yourself. Don't write down the things you don't like: doing this gives them an energy we don't want them to have; it's enough that you have named them. But do write down what you like about your life and about yourself and any positives you'd like to add. Focus your energies on these positive aspects of you, so that they become who and what you want to be and live your life the way you want to live it.

Caroline Myss not only stresses the importance of this stage, but also lets us know what we are doing. We are re-creating ourselves, the way that we want to be, and we are choosing our own boundaries. From here on in we 'evolve' the way we want to. It may entail a few steps forward and a few steps back, but the way is always forward, we never lose the ground we've gained. It may seem like it sometimes, but that feeling is only temporary. This journey of self-discovery, taking back your life, is hard work, there is no doubt about that. But it is the best work you'll ever do. It is an adventure, one that lasts a lifetime, and once you have embarked on it you will never want to give up on it.

In his book, *The One Quest*, Claudio Naranjo, described as the most influential figure in Latin American Gestalt therapy, stressed that the most important qualification for anyone who aspired to help others was their personal development. He wrote '… it seems that no qualification for the one in the helping position is more crucial than the degree of his own personal development.' [7] So I think it's fair to say that if this is a 'crucial' commitment from the therapist, how much more crucial is this commitment from all of us who touch the lives of children in any way?

SELF-AWARENESS: THE KEY TO FULFILMENT – SUMMARIES

◆ 'First know thyself' – self-awareness is the key.
◆ The problem of being human.
◆ Without self-awareness we can pass our wounds onto our children.
◆ We must be aware of our impact on other people's lives.

- ◆ Outwardly adult, many of us are carrying a wounded child inside.
- ◆ Many of us have internalised a wounding critical voice.
- ◆ We have to contact and heal our inner child.
- ◆ We have to know what motivates us and why we react the way we do in certain circumstances.
- ◆ What predominant messages did we receive as children? Were they nurturing or punitive? Did they help or hinder us?
- ◆ What conflicts do our wounds create in us?
- ◆ Self-esteem is fundamental to a happy, successful life.
- ◆ A guide to changing our conditioning.
- ◆ Our personal development is a crucial commitment.

13

RE-PARENTING
Be the Parent You Always Wanted to Be

'... if parents are to receive the insightful help that will enable them to become the good parents they seek to be, a much greater understanding of unconscious conflict and its role in creating disturbances in the parent's management of their children will have to be achieved...'

Bowlby

'Human life proceeds from a relationship. It can only subsist through relationships. It can only develop in contact with affective relationships, that is, relationships in which it draws affection and warmth, where it encounters deep and positive sentiments of others in respect to oneself.'

PRH

Contact with *affective* relationships emphasises the basic need in all of us, in every newborn and developing individual, for a containing, loving relationship in which to flourish. An affective relationship is one where we are nurtured by affection and warmth and where we encounter positive feedback about our being in the world. Without this positive feedback, we can experience overwhelming feelings, such as those described by Jungian analyst Rose-Emily Rothenberg, of 'a profound sense of unworthiness', a 'feeling of guilt', and 'a profound pull toward death.' [3] All of which I can relate to, as these feelings haunted me until my experience of grief. Without such an experience or successful therapy, or some life changing situation, we can carry these feelings throughout life, not realising why and where they originated. We can be crippled by them and pass these wounds on to the next generation.

ACKNOWLEDGING MISTAKES

It has been said that, unless a parent can acknowledge their mistakes, the process of healing cannot start for the child, whatever age their 'child' is. There has to be some attempt at acknowledgement on the part of the parent. This isn't easy for us to do, but it is a crucial part of reparation. We need to be honest with ourselves about the sort of parent we were. I can't emphasise enough that this isn't about blame. It's about *taking responsibility for putting things right in so far as we can where needed*, which is very different. It is about looking honestly at the circumstances of our lives with our children and asking ourselves what they truly were. Many things were beyond our control. The emotional deficit from our own childhood will have had a major influence on how we were. Also important is the support system that was around us when we had our children because this can make such a difference to how we are able to nurture our baby. Often the instinctive mother, if she has survived at all, gets all but drowned out. Sadly too, fathers can get in the way of the bond between the mother and baby if their 'unconscious conflicts' resulting from deficits in their own childhoods get in the way.

So many things will have been beyond our control, especially if our own experiences were less than adequate or helpful to our own development. Re-parenting isn't about blaming ourselves, our parents or their parents. The cycles go back endlessly. Rather, it's about being honest with ourselves, so that we can begin the work of being the parent we would have liked to have been had our own circumstances been different. Never before has the old adage 'better late than never' been more true or more important.

Although I don't think we can ever give back to our children what we took from them because of our own lack (sadly they have to do their own retrieval work), we can nevertheless help them on their healing path by being the parent we could and should have been, had our own circumstances been different.

FAMILY DYNAMICS

If we willingly do the necessary work – and I don't pretend it's easy (that old Japanese proverb comes to mind, 'Fall down seven times, get up eight') – by healing and changing ourselves our family dynamics will change too. Some people will welcome the newly emerging 'you'. Others will not, because the new you doesn't fit their own agendas. But all that we are concerned with here is our relationship with our children, the inheritors of our wounded selves.

It is important to remember though, that as you change, moving closer to being the parent you want to be, even though your children will welcome these changes, they have been 'programmed' by the 'old you'. I sometimes realise that my children are reacting to something I've said or done as if I were the 'old' me. It is an uncomfortable reminder of how I used to be but I'm still thankful that I've changed. I no longer have to be the critical, short-fused mother I once was, who lived so much of the time out of her childhood wounding.

Now there is only one thing I ask of them, the only thing that any parent has the right to ask of their child. Quite simply I want them to be happy. Happy within their own lives. Lives lived as they wish to live them. I am no longer trying to fit them into my idea of what's right for them. I no longer think I know better than they do what's good for them. One of the things we learn during our training as counsellors is that at some level the client not only knows what's wrong, they also know what they need to put it right. The counselling process helps to draw this 'knowing' out for them. The same applies to our children's lives. Somewhere in their psyche they know what and where their path lies and how to fulfil it. 'The issue is not so much what parents give to them as what they don't take away.' (4)

It's very important that we don't get in their way. Or if we already have, since we are talking about re-parenting here, we do all we can to get out of their way now and put right what we can.

MAKING CHANGES

The message of this chapter is a simple one. The solution is simple too. You can start straight away being the parent you would have liked to have been. It simply requires you to look at how you were and now are, with your children, regardless of their age, and to think about how you would have liked to have been had things been different and what sort of relationship you would like to have with them now and to start creating it. Adler's suggestion to 'act as if' comes to mind here. We need to work on ourselves, understanding what makes us respond to people and events the way we do. This isn't accomplished overnight of course, but the very fact that we want to do it will begin to have positive results.

We must begin to really see our children. See *them* as they truly are, not just what we want to see. We must be attentive and accepting. We must accept that what we see and don't like is probably of our making. Over half a century ago Jung wrote, 'Parents should always be conscious of the fact that they themselves are the principle cause of neurosis in their children.' However, seeing the wider picture, he also wrote, 'It is not so much the parents as their ancestors – the grandparents and great-grandparents – who are the true progenitors.' (5)

So the damage isn't all down to us, but the reparation is, because, regardless of who the main progenitors are, the buck stops with us. More importantly, that is also where the healing starts so that *healing and well-being get passed down the generations*, rather than ancient wounds.

One of the results that we are aiming for is for our child not to 'need' us and for us not to 'need' them. There are a lot of needy parents who won't let the child grow up or grow away. There are other parents who push their children out even before they can walk. Yet others paradoxically do both at the same time.

Needy parents, the ones who live through their children, should, for their own sakes and for the sake of their child, make the effort to get a life of their own. Parents who perhaps didn't really want to have children and who push their children out as soon as possible, if not sooner, need to think about what they are doing and why they are doing it, before forfeiting the most precious thing they possess. Parents that do both at the same time are parents that at one level resent their children but need them in their lives, perhaps to shore up a less than satisfying relationship or to mitigate what would otherwise be a lonely, friendless life. Needless to say, none of this is helpful to the children involved, whatever age those children are.

However, what we did or didn't do isn't the issue. It doesn't matter. It is academic. It's what we do now that's important. It could be a matter of life or death, literally or psychologically. And the most important thing we can do is to respect and value our child for himself or herself. There are few things more potent for any of us, but especially for our child, whatever his or her age, than to be respected and valued by us, for the unique individual they are. As Scott Peck said, 'The feeling of being valuable – "I am a valuable person" – is essential to mental health and is a cornerstone of self-discipline. It is a direct product of parental love. Such a conviction must be gained in childhood; it is extremely difficult to acquire it during adulthood.' (6)

It is difficult to acquire the feeling of being valuable during adulthood, *but it is possible.* Listen to what your children say about their feelings, both feelings felt in the present and feelings from their childhood. However difficult it is for us to accept these feelings, they are a gift of healing, for us and our child. Even if we don't fully understand where these feelings are coming from, at least we must be willing to try and understand and accept that this is how it was for them. How they experienced life with us. Bruno Bettelheim stresses the importance of letting our child truly express their feelings when he writes that it is only after children no longer need to repress negative feelings about their parents, that they can experience a loving relationship with them.

Above all, we must take what our child says seriously. Wherever we are in our own growth, we can begin our re-parenting, begin being the parent we would have liked to have been, respecting and valuing the genuine self of our child. Relating to our child with respect for the unique individual they are is a sure and certain way to render even simple thoughtlessness, in any of its forms, impossible. So is deciding to do the work of re-parenting, which asks that we love and accept ourselves and make a commitment to a growing self-awareness.

Admittedly it is a lifelong task, which can, at times, be painful, but the rewards along the way are endless. As I explained in an earlier chapter, one of the tasks we have to do is to listen, accept and take seriously our inner child, the holder of all our childhood pain. It is vital that we get to know this part of ourselves because our dormant wounds and even the wounds we think we know about, are a tremendous source of discomfort. Events or remarks can touch this place in us and at times make us act in ways we can come to regret. Psychotherapist Samuel Osherson says that if we haven't done our own healing work our wounds come between ourselves and everyone else and this is especially true in regard to ourselves and our children.

Strategy: Taking your child seriously and relating to them as a unique individual as you would have done if circumstances had been different for you:

- The first and crucial step is to see the need and to want to make changes.
- Decide how you would have liked to have been and decide to be that way now.
- Take seriously the need to heal your own wounds and do your own self-awareness work.
- Be honest with yourself as to how you were/are with your child and how that has impacted their life.
- Let go of preconceived ideas about how your child should/ could be.
- Accept that what you might not like in your child could be a reflection of yourself or of your making.
- Listen to your child and take seriously how they experienced their childhood. It's how it was for them that matters and needs to be heard.
- Respect and value them for who and what they are.
- Be attentive and accepting without judgement and with gratitude.
- This is an ongoing process. Healing your own life goes hand in hand with nurturing your relationship with your child.
- This isn't about blame. It's about doing something truly worth doing for everyone involved now and for future generations

The prognosis is good though because there are plenty of books available and workshops we can go to in these more enlightened times, and you will be surprised by the results for yourself, your children and all your relationships. Remember, this work is better done late than never at all and is just as relevant to your child, whatever their age, to them and their inner child and of course their own children, your grandchildren and all the generations that will follow.

RE-PARENTING: BE THE PARENT YOU ALWAYS WANTED TO BE – SUMMARIES

◆ Every child is entitled to a containing, loving relationship in which to flourish.
◆ We need positive feedback about our being in the world.
◆ Parents need to be able to acknowledge their mistakes.
◆ This isn't about blame.
◆ Our own emotional deficit will have played a part in our ability to parent.
◆ Fathers need to protect the bond between mother and baby.
◆ The early bonding a baby experiences is crucially important.
◆ Our children are the inheritors of our own wounds.
◆ All we can ask of our children is that they are happy.
◆ You can start straight away being the parent you would have liked to have been had things been different for you.
◆ We need to work on our wounds. This alone will bring positive results.
◆ It's what we do now that matters.
◆ We must respect and value our child for his/her self.
◆ We must take what our child says seriously.
◆ We must also accept and take seriously our inner child too.
◆ Our efforts will benefit ourselves, our children, grandchildren and all future generations.

14

....

WHY BORN
BEAUTIFUL?

'…we do have much information that is necessary to all but
it is in the hands of a few.'

Virginia Satir

This quote from Virginia Satir is exactly why I wanted to write
this book. In my final year at university as a mature student, I
studied the philosophy of psychopathology and there I found
writers, some of whom are quoted here, talking about the things
I had learnt the hard way, intuitively and with much soul searching, over many years. It felt like a sort of betrayal that this
knowledge had gone round and round in academia and not got
to where it was needed – in the public domain, where it could
make a difference.

But what is making a difference now are the many books that
have been written in recent years, uncovering the painful and
unhappy lives of their authors when they were children. They
speak for legions of children whose stories will never be told. The
fact that these children, as adults, can speak as they have about
their childhood experiences is a reminder, as I've said before, that

we are never alone with a child. A child's adult sees and hears everything that is done to them; nothing is forgotten. We can and must do better. It is the responsibility of every parent and adult to be the best they can be, so giving the children whose lives they touch the best possible start in adult life.

The final quote belongs to Philip Larkin, a perceptive and insightful poet who poignantly wrote:

> 'In everyone there sleeps
> A sense of life lived according to love.
> To some it means the difference they could make
> By loving others, but across most it sweeps
> As all they might have done had they been loved.' [2]

The next line says; 'That nothing cures' but I haven't included it in the quote above because I don't believe it. There is always hope. I have never gone into a session with a client, however dire the circumstances, without hope in my heart for a successful outcome, eventually. And there is a cure: kindness, acceptance, warmth, positive regard, empathy, (many of the qualities indispensable to Carl Rogers) – any one of these can undo the harm of thoughtless or unkind treatment and begin the healing process.

The more I look into the faces of babies and young children, the more I see that they are all born beautiful. That is the message of this book. People aren't born drug addicts, thieves or murderers. Babies aren't born suffering, because it is suffering from the many pathologies that beset and stifle lives. Buddhists believe that a pathology, a sickness of the mind, happens as a result of unacceptable pressure being put on a person to be different from their true nature. This pressure, to be something other than we truly are, can begin at birth and gather momentum as we progress through baby-hood, infancy, childhood and adolescence.

Again, I want to stress that this isn't about blame; it's about looking honestly at the facts. The fact is that a child's potential as an adult, that is his or her ability to be fulfilled emotionally, psychologically, physically and spiritually, is dependent on the quality of care received in the early years in particular, and throughout childhood.

We as adults cannot escape the fact that, whether as parents, carers, relatives, teachers, nurses, doctors, shop assistants (the list is endless), with every child's life we touch, we will have an impact. We will have an effect on that child's emotional well-being, which in turn impacts their overall mental health. As long as this truth is comfortably out of awareness, people don't have to take it on board, and the harm continues from generation to generation. But so much is now known and it is time that what is known has a bene-ficial effect on our lives, both as individuals and on our society as a whole. Of course, events over which no one has any control also play a part, but how a person feels about themselves in the inner self determines how they cope with these outer influences.

Our children are a reflection of ourselves, of the society they live in, which is of our making, not theirs. Respect is possibly the most important quality we can nurture in ourselves and in our children. When we have respect we take responsibility for the way we are in the world, how our being affects the lives of others. It is closely allied to love, by which I mean caring, compassion and common sense. All of which would make our lives and our streets much happier and safer places to live.

'All the children who are held and loved… will know how to love others. Spread these virtues in the world. Nothing more need be done.'

Mengzi, c.300 BC

WHY BORN BEAUTIFUL? – SUMMARIES

◆ We cannot benefit from knowledge that just goes round and round in academia.

◆ We are never alone with a child. Their adult self hears and sees everything.

◆ There is always hope.

◆ Children are born beautiful.

◆ The pressure to be something other than we truly are can begin at birth.

◆ This isn't about blame.

◆ The quality of care in infancy will have an influence on a child's emotional health.

◆ Every child's life we touch we will impact in some way.

◆ Our children are a reflection of something in ourselves.

◆ Respect is so important.

◆ Caring, compassion and common sense are closely allied to love.

ACKNOWLEDGEMENTS

I would like to say thank you to:

Richard, my good companion of fifty two years.

My children.

Neve, our youngest granddaughter, for being the catalyst for *Born Beautiful*.

All our grandchildren, for the fun and joy they've brought into our lives.

Wendy, for helping me clarify my path.

Everyone, whose kindness down the years has helped me on my healing journey.

And Alice and Lisa at Free Association Books, for their sensitive professionalism.

COPYRIGHT
PERMISSIONS

Abrams, Jeremiah – *Reclaiming the Inner Child* – Reproduced by kind permission from the author.

Bowlby, John – *The Making and Breaking of Affectional Bonds* – By kind permission of the Taylor & Francis Group

Burks, Fred – *Peers Website* – By kind permission from the author.

Cardinal, Marie – *The Words to Say It* – By kind permission of The Women's Press.

Chopra, Deepak – *Ageless Body Timeless Mind* – (Published by Ebury) By kind permission of The Random House Group Ltd c2005

Coelho, Paulo – *By the River Piedra I Sat Down and Wept* – By permission of HarperCollins Publishers Ltd cPaulo Coelho 2014

Cooper, Cassie – *Psychodynamic therapy: the Kleinian approach* in *Individual Therapy* – By kind permission of Sage Publishing.

Cooper, Diana – *A Little Light on the Spiritual Laws* – By kind permission of Hodder & Stoughton.

Daniels, V. & Horowitz, L. – *Being and Caring* – By kind permission from the authors.

De Mello, Anthony – *Awareness* – By kind permission of Zondervan Publishing.

Ferenczi, Sandor – *The Clinical Diaries of Sandor Ferenczi* – By kind permission of The Marsh Agency Ltd., for Judith Dupont on behalf of The Estate of Sandor Ferenczi.

Foundation for Inner Peace – *A Course In Miracles* – By kind permission of The Foundation for Inner Peace CA 94949

Gibran, Kahlil – *The Eye of the Prophet* – By kind permission of Profile Books.

Goleman, Daniel – *Emotional Intelligence* – By kind permission of Bloomsbury Publishing Plc.

Hudson, Kerry – *Lowborn* – Reprinted by kind permission of The Random House Group Limited.

Jung, Carl – *Collected Works Vol 17* – By kind permission of Princeton University Press.

Larkin, Philip – *The Whitsun Weddings* – By kind permission of Faber & Faber Ltd.

Lewis, C.S. – *A Grief Observed* – By kind permission of Faber & Faber Ltd.

Longley, Clifford – *Article in the Daily telegraph* – With kind permission from Telegraph Media Group Limited.

McCaffry, Annie – *Journey to Myself* – By kind permission from the author.

Marooney, Kimberly – *Angel Blessings* – By kind permission of Fair Winds Publishing Quarto Group.

Metzner, Ralph – *The Unfolding Self* – By kind permission from The Green Earth Foundation.

Naranjo, Claudio – *The One Quest* – By kind permission of Gateway Books & Tapes, California

O'Neill, Onora Prof. – *'Children's Rights and children's Lives* – By kind permission of the University of Chicago Press.

Peck, M. Scott – *The Road Less Travelled* – Published by Arrow reproduced by kind permission of The Random House Group Ltd. c1990

PRH – *Persons and their Growth* – By kind permission of Personality and Human Relations International

Rosenberg, Marshall B. Ph.D. – *Nonviolent Communication: A Language of Life* Reprinted with kind permission from The Puddle Dancer Press.

Rothenberg, Rose-Emily – *'The Orphan Archetype'* By kind permission from the author.

Ruiz, Don Miguel – *The Four Agreements* – By kind permission of Amber-Allen Publishing.

Sangster, W.E. – *Daily readings from W.E. Sangster* – By kind permission of the author's family.

Satir, Virginia – *People Making* – By kind permission of Profile Books.

Short, Susanne – *The Whispering of the Walls* – By kind permission from the author.

Stevens, Barry – *Person To Person* – By kind permission of Real People Press.

Symington, Neville – *The Analytic Experience* – By kind permission of Free Association Books.

The Dalai Lama – *The Dalai Lama's Book of Love and Compassion* – By kind permission of HarperCollins Publishers Ltd.

Warner, Jenny – *Adlerian therapy* in *Individual Therapy* – By kind permission of Sage Publishing.

Winnicott, D.W. – *The Child the Family and the Outside World* – By kind permission of the Marsh Agency Ltd..

World Goodwill – *Gifts of Youth, Gifts of Age* – By kind permission of The Lucis Trust, London.

Excerpts from "Oedipus: The 'Guilty' Victim" from THOU SHALT NOT BE AWARE by Alice Miller, translated by Hildegarde and Hunter Hannum. Translation copyright © 1984 by Alice Miller. Used/Reprinted by permission of Farrar, Straus and Giroux.

BIBLIOGRAPHY

Foreword

Bowlby, John, *The Making and Breaking of Affectional Bonds* (Routledge) 1979 p.21

Stevens, Barry, (with Carl Rogers) *Person to Person* (Souvenir Press) 1973 p.177

Introduction

Daniels, V. & Horowitz, L.J. *Being and Caring* (San Francisco Book Company) 1976 p.93

Chapter 1: How Counselling Can Enrich Our Parenting

Cooper, Cassie, *Individual Therapy* (Ed.) Dryden, W. (Open University Press) 1990 p.54

Cooper, C. Ibid. p.54

World Goodwill Newsletter *Gifts of Youth Gifts of Age* (Lucis Trust) 2002 p.3

Larkin, Philip, *The Whitsun Weddings* (Faber & Faber) 1986 p.16

Chapter 2: Education For Life: The Theories

Gardner, Howard, quoted in *Emotional Intelligence* Goleman D. (Bloomsbury Publishing) 1996 p.37

Warner, Jenny, *Individual Therapy* op. cit. p.88

Chapter 3: The Simple Needs of the Baby

Symington, Neville, *The Analytic Experience* (FAB) 1986 p.238

Daniels & Horowitz, *Being and Caring* op. cit. p.322

Burks, Fred, *A Whitehouse Insider's Journey* (Peers Website) 26/7/2019

Metzner, Ralf, *The Unfolding Self* (Origin Press) 1998 p.158

Chapter 4: The Terrific Twos

A Course In Miracles (Foundation for Inner Peace) 1992 p.26

Chopra, Deepak, *Ageless Body Timeless Mind* (Rider) 1993 p.141

Chapter 5: The Maternal Instinct

Gibran, Kahlil, *The Eye of the Prophet* (Souvenir Press) 1995 p.68

Winnicott, W.D. *The Child the Family and the Outside World* (Penguin Books) 1991 p.16

Chapter 6: The Family

Longley, Clifford, *The Daily Telegraph* January 28th 1994 p.19

His Holiness The Dalai Lama, *Book of Love and Compassion* (Thorsons) 2001 p.38

Goleman, Daniel, *Emotional Intelligence* (Bloomsbury Publishing) 1996 p.189

Miller, Alice, *Thou Shalt Not Be Aware* (Farrar, Straus & Giroux) 1984 p.156

Goleman, D. *Emotional Intelligence* op. cit. p.213

Chapter 7: Born Beautiful

Miller, Alice, *Thou Shalt Not Be Aware* Farrar, Straus & Giroux 1984 p.156

McCaffrey, Anne, *Journey to myself* (Element) 1992 p.117

Marooney, K. *Angel Blessings* (Fair Winds Press) 1995 p.52

Chapter 8: Oedipus and Freud Revisited

Ferenczi, S. *The Clinical Diary of Sandor Ferenczi* (Harvard University Press) 1995 p.79

Daniels, V. & Horowitz, L.J. *Being And Caring* op. cit. p.120

Bowlby, J. *The Making and Breaking of Affectional Bonds* op. cit. p.14

Cardinal, Marie, *The Words to Say It* (The Women's Press) 2000 p.68

Cardinal, Marie, Ibid. p.70

Chapter 9: The Importance of Kindness

Sangster, W.E. *Daily Readings from W.E. Sangster* (Epworth Press) 1966 p.327

Larkin, Philip, *The Whitsun Weddings* op. cit. p.15

Prof. O'Neill, O. *Ethics* (1988) p.448

Gibran, K. op. cit. p.69

Lewis, C.S. *A Grief Observed* (Faber & Faber) 1987 p.36

Lewis, C.S. Ibid. p.52

Chapter 10: Compassionate Parenting

Abrams, Jeremiah, *Reclaiming The Inner Child* (Putman) 1990 p.276

Matthew 12: 36–37 (The British Foreign Bible Society) 1844

Rosenberg, Marshall B. *Nonviolent Communication: A Language of Compassion* (Puddle Dancer Press) 1999 p.ii

Bebermeyer, Ruth, from *Nonviolent Communication* Ibid p.27

Abrams, J. *Reclaiming the Inner Child* op. cit. p.9

Hudson, Kerry, *Lowborn* (Penguin Random House UK) 2019 p.47

Chapter 11: Adolescence

Goleman, Daniel, *Emotional Intelligence* op. cit. p.232

Rosenberg, Marshall B. *Nonviolent Communication* op. cit. p.138

Coelho, Paulo, *By the River Piedra I Sat Down and Wept.* (Harper Collins) 2014 p.45

Chapter 12: Self-awareness: The Key to Fulfilment

Bowlby, J. *The Making and Breaking of Affectional Bonds* op. cit. p.16

Ruiz, Don Miguel, *The Four Agreements* (Amber Allen) 1997 p.98–99

Stevens, B. *Person to Person* op. cit. p.9–11

Cooper, Diana, *A Little Light on the Spiritual Laws* (Hodder & Stoughton) 2000 p.199

De Mello, Anthony, *Awareness* (Zondervan) 1990 p.71

Daniels & Horowitz, *Being And Caring* op. cit. p.270

Naranjo, Claudio, *The One Quest* (Wildwood House London 1974, reprinted Gateway Books California) 2005 p.121

Chapter 13: Re-parenting: Be the Parent You Always Wanted to Be

Bowlby, J. *The Making and Breaking of Affectional Bonds* op. cit. p.20

PRH, *Persons and Their Growth* (Personality and Human Relations) 1997, 3rd printing 2007 p.127

Rothenberg, Rose-Emily, *Reclaiming the Inner Child* (Putman) 1990 p.91–93

Short, Susanne, Ibid. p.202

Jung, C.G. quoted in *Reclaiming the Inner Child* (Putman) 1990 p.122

Peck, Scot, *The Road Less Travelled* (Arrow) 1990 p.23

Chapter 14: Why Born Beautiful?

Satir, Virginia, *People Making* (Souvenir Press) 1994 p.207

Larkin, Philip, *The Whitsun Weddings* op. cit. p.15